D0250679

In This House,
We Will
Giggle

Praise for
In This House, We Will Giggle

"Every parent needs this book! I love Courtney's fun, practical ways to connect our kids with biblical truth while making family memories. This book is an amazing resource that will teach children how to have their own relationship with God."

—LYSA TERKEURST, *New York Times* best-selling author
and president of Proverbs 31 Ministries

"Courtney DeFeo has written the book I wish I'd had while my kids were growing up! It's full of creativity and fun for anchoring twelve key virtues into the hearts of children. I love how her ideas lay a vital foundation for spiritual growth and development—and help families have a blast while doing it."

—SANDRA STANLEY, North Point Ministries

"If you're looking for real-life ways to become a more proactive instead of reactive parent, you should read this book. Courtney DeFeo gives us personalized and practical ideas for building love and laughter into our children so we can actually develop an intentional plan for investing in them."

—REGGIE JOINER, founder and CEO of Orange

"We laughed our way through this book with its honest snapshot of all that comes with being a parent. We also were seriously inspired to invite our kids into a life filled with virtues. Courtney takes the guesswork out of it by giving parents creative and practical ways to seize everyday moments and make following Jesus *fun!*"

—LAUREN TOMLIN, wife of Christian music artist Chris Tomlin
and on the journey with him to raising a family after the
heart of Jesus

"I love being a dad, but to be honest, I'm an insecure one. I want to be really good at this, but there are days when I wonder. This is one of the many reasons I love Courtney's book. She reminds us that we should take parenting seriously, but not so much ourselves. Love, giggles, and virtues are a lot more fun than perfection anyway. This is a practical and encouraging guide for parents who aren't perfect but who want to get this extraordinary opportunity right—and have fun along the way."

—Jeff Henderson, lead pastor of Gwinnett Church,
dad to Jesse and Cole, and husband of Wendy

"As a counselor, I hear weary parents every day trying to figure out how to combat the entitlement of this generation, instill virtues in their children, and enjoy one another at the same time. I'm so grateful for this book, which contains encouragement and practical ideas to do just that! Your family will be inspired to grow, serve, love, and laugh together!"

—Sissy Goff, director of child and adolescent counseling at
Daystar Counseling Ministries, Nashville, TN, and author
of several books, including *Intentional Parenting*

"Courtney DeFeo, in her typical style, offers us something refreshingly different, powerful, and creative: a secret weapon for parents. For me this book felt like the Swiss Army Knife of parenting, with a tool just waiting to be applied as needed to every occasion…with a dose of fun and giggles along the way!"

—David Salyers, vice president of marketing for Chick-fil-A Inc.
and coauthor of *Remarkable!*

"Every mother will be helped by this practical, inspirational, and down-to-earth book. Each page holds biblical truth, family-time suggestions, and a huge trunk full of plans to help you teach twelve beautiful virtues. If you choose to do as this book suggests, your family is in for a lovely journey."

—Esther Burroughs, author and speaker with Esther
Burroughs Ministries, Greenville, SC

"Like Courtney, I want to create a home where our children experience Christ in a tangible way. The ideas in this book are practical, and the stories are relatable. You'll come away with fresh inspiration for nurturing a faith-filled, fun-loving family."

—Holly Furtick, author of *The Preacher's Wife* blog and wife
of Pastor Steven Furtick, Elevation Church, Charlotte, NC

In This House, We Will Giggle

Making **VIRTUES,**
LOVE & **LAUGHTER**
a Daily Part of
YOUR FAMILY LIFE

Courtney DeFeo

WATERBROOK
PRESS

IN THIS HOUSE, WE WILL GIGGLE
PUBLISHED BY WATERBROOK PRESS
12265 Oracle Boulevard, Suite 200
Colorado Springs, Colorado 80921

All Scripture quotations, unless otherwise indicated, are taken from the Holy Bible, New International Version®, NIV®. Copyright © 1973, 1978, 1984, 2011 by Biblica Inc.™ Used by permission of Zondervan. All rights reserved worldwide. www.zondervan.com. Scripture quotations marked (MSG) are taken from The Message by Eugene H. Peterson. Copyright © 1993, 1994, 1995, 1996, 2000, 2001, 2002. Used by permission of NavPress Publishing Group. All rights reserved. Scripture quotations marked (NASB) are taken from the New American Standard Bible®. © Copyright The Lockman Foundation 1960, 1962, 1963, 1968, 1971, 1972, 1973, 1975, 1977, 1995. Used by permission. (www.Lockman.org). Scripture quotations marked (NKJV) are taken from the New King James Version®. Copyright © 1982 by Thomas Nelson Inc. Used by permission. All rights reserved. Scripture quotations marked (NLT) are taken from the Holy Bible, New Living Translation, copyright © 1996, 2004, 2007. Used by permission of Tyndale House Publishers Inc., Carol Stream, Illinois 60188. All rights reserved.

Trade Paperback ISBN 978-1-60142-606-2
eBook ISBN 978-1-60142-607-9

Copyright © 2014 by Courtney DeFeo

Cover design by Kelly L. Howard

All rights reserved. No part of this book may be reproduced or transmitted in any form or by any means, electronic or mechanical, including photocopying and recording, or by any information storage and retrieval system, without permission in writing from the publisher.

Published in the United States by WaterBrook Multnomah, an imprint of the Crown Publishing Group, a division of Penguin Random House LLC, New York.

WATERBROOK and its deer colophon are registered trademarks of Penguin Random House LLC.

Library of Congress Cataloging-in-Publication Data
DeFeo, Courtney.
  In this house, we will giggle : making virtues, love, and laughter a daily part of your family life / Courtney DeFeo. — First Edition.
      pages cm
  Includes bibliographical references.
  ISBN 978-1-60142-606-2 — ISBN 978-1-60142-607-9 (electronic) 1. Christian education—Home training. 2. Christian education of children. 3. Laughter—Religious aspects—Christianity. 4. Families—Religious aspects—Christianity. I. Title.
  BV1590.D44 2014
  248.8'431—dc23

                                                          2014021156

Printed in the United States of America
2016

10 9 8 7 6 5

SPECIAL SALES
Most WaterBrook Multnomah books are available at special quantity discounts when purchased in bulk by corporations, organizations, and special-interest groups. Custom imprinting or excerpting can also be done to fit special needs. For information, please e-mail SpecialMarkets @WaterBrookMultnomah.com or call 1-800-603-7051.

To Ron, Ella, and Larson:
You have shown me a love and laughter
that I never knew was possible.
In this house, I will treasure you.

Contents

Why *Giggle* in This House?

Before my two girls came along, I had a vision for my home. I wanted it to look very similar to the home in which I grew up—full of life and joy. A house of love. A place where my children would feel welcome even when *every single toy* was not put away. Where they would feel free to be themselves and even to make a mistake or mess up.

In my ideal vision of home, each member of the family feels accepted no matter what. There's a lot of running and playing. You may hear an occasional word of correction or see a rule enforced, but all is covered with love and grace. If you peek inside those children's hearts, you see them yearning to be just like their mom and dad. They are excited to grow up but anxious to return home to make more memories. And the sound that rings throughout that crazy house? Giggles!

That's what I had planned for our family home: love and grace, memory making and giggles.

And then I had kids.

Some harsh reality came my way. Instead of giggles, critical words often echoed in our home. On some days, it felt more sterile than warm. Everything might be scheduled and organized, but smiles were fading.

Despite my early hopes, my home felt little like the one I'd envisioned—and a lot like the houses of fear I'd witnessed while growing up. In those homes, emotional tension and a lot of rules led to a sense of nervousness and fear. You could almost hear the Von Trapp family whistle calling everyone to scurry and line up for instructions. If you could peek inside these kids' minds and hearts, you might observe them counting the days until their release from that home.

What a heartbreaking situation, and certainly not what I wanted for my family. Over time, my husband and I realized we wanted to make some changes. We began to loosen up on the schedule and noticed that everyone's heart became lighter. We became less concerned about behavior enforcement and more interested in heart development—and we saw love and delight blossom in our home. And while we absolutely believe in the value of discipline and guidance, we started looking for fun, enjoyable ways to teach our children what matters most. As we daily make choices to lean toward love and giggles, our home is becoming much more like the one I dreamed of before I became a mom.

How about you? Which sort of home did you grow up in?

When you think about God and how you view Him, is He like the parents in the first home or the second?

Which home and view of Christ do you want for your kids?

Do you believe the joyful home is even possible?

I have to tell you, I'm convinced it is. And this book is all about taking steps to make that joyful home a reality for all of us.

The Toughest Job We'll Ever Love

The day I held my first baby girl in my arms, questions began swirling in my head. *What kind of home will we give her? Will she enjoy us? Will we hurt her? Will she always trust us?* My husband and I have made it our pursuit to create the first home, the fun and loving home. A home where grace and love flow. A home where kids see Christ's love in action. A home where giggles—not screams—erupt through the windows.

Pursuit means that our family has not arrived. In fact, we will never fully arrive. I am not a perfect mom. I am not a supermom. And as a recovering perfectionist, I know I am dependent on my Savior. I need Him desperately. Daily. This job of raising children is the toughest thing I have ever attempted. It is also the most exciting, the most liberating, and the most fulfilling call I have ever experienced.

My girls, Ella and Larson, are not my whole world, but they are worth giving my best effort for my whole life. If I do my part well, they could grow up to lead a nation, a small group, a church, a family, or a class of students. They could change another's heart for Christ, they could lend a helping hand, or they could start a movement. They could serve their husbands and raise precious children.

If I dwell on the huge responsibility of being a parent, it could freeze me with fear. However, I choose not to let worry stop me and I dive in, knowing that if I fail or mess up, I am always getting back up. Our best moments as a family can often be found in the mess of life, not in the planned or perfect.

In those moments when I begin to feel overwhelmed, I remember these children are not totally mine. They are held and loved by the God who created the universe. He knows them, and He knows best exactly what they are designed to do. He has a story, and they have a place in it. I have the massive privilege of opening their eyes to this story and showing them options and possibilities for glorifying His name.

Trust me, I fight a daily battle between my natural self and the mom I want to be. All too often I lose sight of my true priorities. I am a controller and perfectionist to my core. There are days I simply want the calm, orderly peace of everyone quietly marching like ducks behind Mom. On those days, my girls are behaving just so Mom does not flip her lid, and they may resemble the robot children in the house of fear. Then, thankfully there is a nudge and a soft whisper: *Loosen up. Don't miss this.* I believe it is my heavenly Father working in me and growing me as a mom, reminding me that the house of love and grace includes mess.

I have seen these messy moments turn into priceless treasures. I see the spark in my children's eyes or the perfect spot to tickle, and we relish a moment and simply giggle. As my beautiful mentor told me, "You'll only pass this way once."

The challenge I face is in holding the right view of my tasks and challenges amid the daily grind. Can I break out of autopilot mode and see beyond my role as an enforcer? Can I seize the teachable moments in each day for the purpose of raising virtuous kids without raising fearful kids? Prompting obedience "because I said so" may pay off in the short term; however, I don't want my children to obey only because they fear consequences or worry that Mom will lose it. I want to know their hearts understand and grasp the joy to be found in doing the right thing. This requires parenting through the daily grind with a long-term mentality.

It's easy to lose perspective and sink into thinking of my job as a mom as nothing more than the relentless changing of dirty diapers, the wiping of snotty noses, and the making of lunches. Can you relate to this despair? But when I look at things from God's high and holy view of motherhood, I can choose to see it all as a thrilling call, a disciple-making job—teaching my kids to live out virtues like joy, love, gratitude, generosity, and patience. My goal is that they feel the joy of Christ's love and learn to walk with Him from the earliest age. When I view my many tasks as a mother from this perspective, it makes the day pretty simple: let me show them Jesus in a very real, personal way. In a delightful way.

Getting Serious About Letting Loose

Did you know that dancing mends a wounded spirit? Did you know giggling and tickling teach love? Did you know a silly family game reminds our kids they have happily married parents? Did you know having family fun and sprinkling in virtues seal lessons into children's hearts for a lifetime?

In his heartwarming book *The Most Important Place on Earth,* Robert Wolgemuth describes all the pieces to the puzzle of a Christian home, and then he echoes my heart for home. "But with all these good things, there is something else I now believe is a vital piece of the Christian home puzzle. It's the serious business of laughter."[1]

Our home, and the environment we create within our family, sets up the impression our kids will have of faith and God. Will they believe Jesus loves only well-behaved, model children, or will they know He loves them just as they are? Will they see the Christian life as a series of rules to be followed, or will they follow Jesus because they've learned from us what it means to love Him and find joy in being with Him?

I believe the Bible very simply describes the fullness of joy found in life with God:

> You will make known to me the path of life;
> In Your presence is fullness of joy;
> In Your right hand there are pleasures forever.
> (Psalm 16:11, NASB)

The joy found in life with God is an "aha" moment for kids and adults alike. When together as a family we awaken to pleasures of loving and following Him, the experience bonds us. When we realize that—no matter our age, gifts, or limitations—we can be used to change others' lives, we are inspired to create family moments that are fun and memorable. Such moments build on each other to create a home kids will want to run back to, not run away from, as soon as they are old enough to choose. This environment makes faith feel less like a burden and more like a privilege. A pleasure.

I'm convinced we can let loose and enjoy our family even as we're teaching profound principles for life. This love-and-laughter approach to spiritual growth is a lot like how we encourage healthy physical growth. We want our kids to choose exercise and healthy foods, but if we constantly lecture them about the benefits of a healthy diet and yell at them for eating junk food, odds are they won't be excited about following our suggestions.

Let's apply this to faith. What if, just as we encourage a toddler to try a new flavor, we invited our kids to taste and see that God is good? that serving Him is actually fun? Instead of telling them to be more generous, let's help them experience for themselves that giving to others feels good and it honors God. Once our kids' perspective turns from "we have to do this" to "we want to do this," they begin making their faith their own. It becomes *who* they are, not *what* they do. A choice over a mandate.

So, on one hand, let's have fun and lighten up and get out the silly string and air guitars. Let's be intentional about creating an environment of affection and joy in our home. Let's close up our computers and ride bikes more often. And at the same time, let's not waste a single opportunity to teach our kids to live out the virtues that can shape their hearts. They live in our homes for only a brief moment, but the lessons they learn and the love they experience will travel with them all their lives. So let's lighten up and get serious. Both. And.

What Are Virtues, Anyway?

So are you ready to dive in and develop a household of love and grace, virtue and giggles? If so, you've probably got some questions like these: *Where do we start? How do we instill what matters most in an engaging way so that we shut the door on the robotic house and open the door to the fun house? What will we use to teach truth that transforms young minds and settles deep into their hearts?*

This book combines three key ingredients—virtues, love, and laughter—in a variety of recipes for creating memorable experiences in your home. Our goal is fewer lectures from us, less eyeball rolling from the kids, and more adventures, more giggles for everyone.

Virtues: what we are teaching

Love & Laughter: how we are teaching

According to *Oxford Dictionaries* online, a virtue is "a quality considered morally good or desirable in a person." So our goal is to teach our children a core set of traits that we value most and desire to see them live out daily—traits you often find referenced on those clever "House Rules" signs, such as love, generosity, service, and responsibility. We want to instill these traits in the hearts of our kids so that their characters reflect the heart of their Savior by the time they leave our nest.

Each chapter focuses on one of twelve different virtues. My suggestion is that you center your efforts on each individual virtue for one full month, implementing the suggested activities and tools to reinforce that concept. With this book and one year of commitment, I believe we can help our kids learn and treasure these virtues in their hearts.

Now, if "one year" just turned you off, let me explain. It's not going to take you one full year to read this book or to implement the key ideas in the chapters ahead, but this timeframe gives you room to breathe and live your life. While I've written this with specific calendar months in mind for each virtue, you can do these activities anytime of the year. And it's up to your family how much time to invest and how to adapt the ideas to your home.

Here are the suggested months for each corresponding virtue:

January: **Joy**

February: **Love**

March: **Forgiveness**

April: **Faith**

May: **Patience**

June: **Perseverance**

July: **Respect**

August: **Responsibility**

September: **Service**

October: **Humility**

November: **Gratitude**

December: **Generosity**

Imagine your little ones walking through life with these seeds of biblical truth planted deep in their hearts and budding out of their lives. Imagine them learning through fun activities and engaging conversations what it means to honor God so that they never even noticed it as "virtue lesson time."

That's why I've written this specifically with the goal of creating experiences for our kids. Think less talking and more doing. Each chapter provides details for a family fun activity to reinforce the virtue of the month. In addition, you'll find catch phrases, discussion questions, Scripture memory verses, and virtue definitions to support your teaching efforts. I encourage you to customize all these resources to fit the style and needs of your family, discarding anything that doesn't work and mixing in your own creative ideas.

Throughout the book you'll also find "60 Ways to Bring Out the Giggles"—quick and easy activities for nurturing a sense of fun in your household. As mentioned earlier, I'm challenging us to simultaneously get serious about the virtues we're teaching and lighten up about how we teach them. I know that may sound confusing, but let me assure you the "what" of passing on our faith hasn't changed in thousands of years; we are teaching our kids the same timeless principles of what it looks like to follow Jesus. But just as churches continually look for ways to be more relevant so they can capture the attention and hearts of people, we can do the same for our families. Let's make our homes places where learning to do the right thing is fun and memorable, not a chore and a lecture.

I realize the idea of deliberately designing opportunities to teach virtues in a meaningful way can sound less like fun and more like yet another item for your never-ending to-do list. As a mom of two little girls, I understand where most parents are sitting today. We are wiped out yet yearning for more. The urgent is pushing out important things. What matters in the next ten minutes is pulling us away from what will matter in ten years. That's why I feel compelled to write this book and share my heart.

> Things which matter most must never be at the mercy of things which matter least.
>
> Goethe

My heart is to empower parents and change little lives by sharing what I've discovered through my own efforts to help my family and others fall in love with Jesus. My passion is not to produce good little Christian kids but to help raise a generation of kids to light up the world for His glory. I believe God can use ordinary moms like you and me to reveal our extraordinary God to our children in a meaningful way.

This Book Is Not...

This book is not a compilation of my own insights. While many of the ideas I share in the following pages come from my own experiences as a mom, I pull core principles largely from God's Word and insights from my own childhood. I was raised by imperfect parents who remained dedicated to living out the perfect love of Christ. And they never let go. In our home they shared the goodness of Christ rather than threatening us with the fear of breaking His commands.

I also share illustrations from other parents who have inspired me to be a better mother. I pray that in reading about the struggles and successes of other families, you will find hope and encouragement that you are not alone in your efforts. I pray each chapter will leave you feeling more than capable and never "less than."

This book is not a list of twelve to-dos to heap on guilt. We don't need another book to do that. And it is not a formula: follow these twelve steps and *poof!* your child will be a pastor and save the world. This is a collection of ideas to make teaching virtues easy and fun. Please don't feel you must repeat exactly the ideas and examples you find throughout the book. Instead I encourage you to customize the concepts to fit the recipe of your precious, unique family. You know the DNA of your family, each personality, each quirk, each tendency, and the best family fun idea is one created by you.

Lastly, this book is not solely for the silly families and crafters. I wrote this book for the working mom, the mom searching out her faith, the single mom, the creative mom, and the busy mom. Parents in all seasons are interested in bringing virtues, love, and laughter into their homes. While you may not choose to do everything, you absolutely will find something in these pages that works for you, especially when you make it your own.

Are you ready? I am! And I'll be doing it with you, every step of the way. Let's go forth and giggle. One virtue at a time. And for heaven's sake, do not tell them up front what we are sneaking into the adventure. Just as carrots sometimes make their way into brownies, we will wrap up these lessons in irresistible love and laughter.

Our Prayer as We Start

Dear Lord, this is my heart's desire: to have a home that overflows with Your love because You have loved us. I want my kids to remember a house full of laughter and fun. I want them to remember truth and the goodness of Your Word because they experienced it for themselves, not because they were forced to obey. Lord, I pray today for a teachable spirit for

_____ [insert kids' names]. I pray that I will have patience when a teaching activity doesn't go according to the plan. I pray You will give me discernment and wisdom. Please guide me to Your way for our family. Please protect my schedule and nudge me to focus on the critical task of raising kids who know You rather than being distracted by the urgent tasks of daily life. Thank You for Your grace and forgiveness. When I mess up, give me the courage to get back up and trust You again the next day. I love You. I entrust You with my life and my family's lives. Amen.

Questions to Answer Now and Discuss Later

1. Which best describes your home—the house of giggles or the house of fear?
2. What behaviors could your family stop doing to help create a home of love and grace?
3. What behaviors could your family start doing to help create a home of love and grace?
4. Once your kids are grown, how do you want them to remember your home?
5. Describe the impression of Jesus you want your kids to have.
6. Name one or two homes you know that are fun but where the parents have a way of teaching values and virtues. Describe them. Make notes of what you'd like to replicate.

But if serving the LORD seems undesirable to you, then choose for yourselves this day whom you will serve, whether the gods your ancestors served beyond the Euphrates, or the gods of the Amorites, in whose land you are living. But as for me and my household, we will serve the LORD.

Joshua 24:15

1

Joy

When the Reality of Life Meets a Heart of Gladness

Memory Verse for the Month

A happy heart makes the face cheerful, but heartache crushes the spirit. *Proverbs 15:13*

Four families with eight kids in one house can get very loud, very quickly. On this particular day, as giggles, squeals, and the occasional shouts of *"Mine!"* echoed through the rooms, I could see growing tension on the faces of the other moms. Our shallow breathing and tight voices suggested a tinge of panic. The house held a lot of tiny people to keep happy and entertained for a long weekend.

As the official hostess, chronic control freak, and

veteran people pleaser, I took charge of the situation and headed straight for the CD player. I caught the eyes of my best friend Katie as I moved through the sea of chaos and kids. She knew it was time to do what we do best: create joy. I pressed one finger on the magical triangle-shaped Play button, and familiar praise tunes blared through the house. Eight squabbling, wild kids joined together for one large dance party. Four sets of parents met in the kitchen to provide an approving audience.

Frowns turned to smiles. Stress vanished. Hands clapped. Hips and feet bebopped. Moods lifted. Giggles erupted. Families worshiped.

Joy had transformed the scene, as it always does.

Joy to You and Me

When I asked my Facebook friends "How do you infuse joy in your home?" I was not surprised that the most popular answer by far was

Family Chase.
Pretend you're a
family of gorillas.

"music." From the seven dwarves singing "Whistle While You Work" to Matt Redman's lyrics "Though I walk through the wilderness, blessed be Your name," music's power to bring joy into challenging situations is something we've all experienced. I have the Pandora app (free version) playing on my phone every day for this very reason.

But true joy, the kind we want for our families, goes much deeper than singing and smiles. Kay Warren once observed, "Joy is the settled assurance that God is in control of all the details of my life, the quiet confidence that ultimately everything is going to be all right, and the determined choice to praise God in all things."[2]

Her words describe exactly what I want to see in my household. They remind me how the psalmist declared of God, "Let all who take refuge in you be glad; let them ever sing for joy. Spread your protection over them, that those who love your name may rejoice in you" (Psalm 5:11).

The joy you and I are aiming to instill in our families this month and for years to come is rooted in our firm belief in God's protection, no matter our circumstances. Here's a brief definition to use with your kids:

Joy: choosing to praise God in all things

I love that this definition covers three points I am trying to teach my kids about joy: (1) it is often a choice, (2) praising God recognizes that He is our source, and (3) "all things" means every circumstance—the good and the bad.

House of Joy

I am so thrilled to start this book with *joy* because I truly desire for my kids to fall in love with Jesus Christ. I am creating a home that shows them the pure joy of living in His love. I pray that memories of joy are etched deep in the hearts of my kids. There is certainly a place for fear of God and biblical correction, but does the Creator of the universe delight in His children? You'd better believe it! Is He the only one who can fill them with true joy? a greater joy than this world can ever offer them? Yes! And we, as parents, provide their earliest impression of His greater joy.

John Piper beautifully explains the source of greatest joy.

> The greatest joy is joy in God.... Fullness of joy and eternal joy
> cannot be improved. Nothing is fuller than full, and nothing is
> longer than eternal. And this joy is owing to the presence of God,
> not the accomplishments of man.[3]

We are the role models of this joy for our children. We greet them in the morning and tuck them into bed at night, and as we stand beside them through all the hours in between, we face the choice of whether or not we will demonstrate joy, along with the other virtues discussed in this book. While we're going to look at some fun activities for centering our families on true joy, I believe God most often works on our families by working first through our hearts, our marriages. Then as our kids see His priorities play out in real life, they absorb those lessons naturally. Our kids will catch this joyful bug by what they see in our homes each day. The choices we make when dad gets fired or when a friend gets the car we wanted. From the big to the small reactions, they are watching.

Of course our desires and intentions are one thing. But what happens when our kiddos wake up and need "milk and a waffle, Mom!" within thirty seconds of peeling their little lion heads off the pillow? How does a heart of joy meet the reality of life?

The Not-So-Joyful Reality

As a parent, you likely have experienced pure joy to the point of elation with your children. But you have also experienced the most frustrating days of your life. I suspect most of us find parenting far more stressful and harder than we ever imagined. This stress—and the daily, often hourly, need to correct and corral these busy young people—often undermines our desire to create a home full of joy and love. We don't expect perfection, but we'd prefer that peace and smiles and happiness outnumber the moments of arguing and complaints and pouting. We don't want to take the easy route to happiness, paved with brownies and bribes; we want our children to experience the fullness of joy found in the love of Jesus Christ.

So what's holding us back?

My brother, Drew, a pastor in Atlanta, recently challenged me in one of his messages: "Don't you think Christians should be the happiest, most joyful people around? Why are we so upset?"

Wow. I sat with this question for a while. We have so many reasons to be joyful, and we can start with the fact of eternal life. I believe joy is given by God and is something He wants our families to experience together. When I think of the never-ending list of blessings He has given me, joy fills my heart and I feel compelled to praise Him. Why can't I operate from this place of gratitude every day?

The truth in Drew's message matches the desires of my heart. I should be able to respond in all circumstances with joy simply because I am a child of God. That is something to celebrate. However, when milk spills on the floor for the third time or I find another smelly load in the washer I forgot to change or I hear "Mine!" and "She hit me!" echoing from the playroom, my reaction isn't immediate joy and smiles as I contemplate my blessings. It is too often a huff, a puff, and a not-so-gentle response.

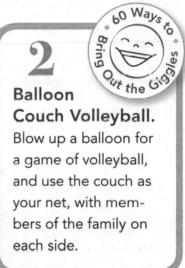

2

60 Ways to Bring Out the Giggles

Balloon Couch Volleyball. Blow up a balloon for a game of volleyball, and use the couch as your net, with members of the family on each side.

Both parents and kids struggle when it comes to choosing joy despite life's little—and big—disappointments.

Just this morning, we had an all-out war at 7 a.m. because I said no to my youngest, Larson, about wearing flip-flops to school. Those are the rules, kid; no flip-flops. She wasn't accepting that answer. Crying, screaming, falling on the floor. When I sent her back upstairs to find a pair of shoes, she resorted to comparing me with her sister, yelling, "You say no to everything! Ella is the nicest person ever! And she says yes to everything!" Alrighty, then. I was highly annoyed. And the day had barely started.

In that moment I decided to make a choice for joy in our home. First, I simply started singing as loudly as I could, " 'I've got the JOY, JOY, JOY, JOY down in my heart.' Where?!" My goal was to shock her out of a tantrum and release my anger in the form of a happy tune instead of yelling. Next, I challenged the girls to a funny-face contest. They had to pop out from behind the wall and make the funniest face they could dream up. We were all giggling in minutes. Larson definitely won the funny-face contest. That kid is hysterical. She forgot about the flip-flops until we got to the car. When she asked again, I stood my ground and gave her two options. She said, "Okay, Moooommm" (drawn out to four syllables and delivered with teenager-like facial expressions). Off we went to school.

60 Ways to Bring Out the Giggles

3

Best Costume Contest.

Let kids dress up in their parents' clothes and accessories.

I'm not always this quick to shift the mood, but I am getting better at not allowing the waves of life to send me crashing. I want to stand firmly on the foundation of God's love and my identity in Him. I am so thankful God has heard my pleas and is helping me learn to keep my perspective and choose gratitude. I do not want to leave a legacy of yelling and snapping. I want my kids to hear me giggle about spills and brush off bad days. I want them to see me have a frustrating moment, apologize, and keep moving forward. The not-so-joyful reality of life confronts us every day. Our kids face it too. Their shiny red balloon escapes into the air, or their favorite friend declares,

"No! I don't want to play with you." Life is tough, for our little ones and our teens, and those lips will sometimes poke out.

In these moments we can be their very best cheerleaders and guide them back to our source of joy. We can continue to remind them that the pursuit of happiness will leave them with an empty heart. The happiness promised by the things of this world is always fleeting. The pursuit of joy found in Christ fills our souls. It is eternal and everlasting.

Breaking the Cycle

I have to confess, I am not a naturally joyful person. My husband, Ron, on the other hand, exudes joy. I often wonder how the Queen of Moods managed to marry Santa Claus. Seriously, I wake up every day next to the jolliest man on earth. By 7 a.m., this man is skipping through the kitchen, hugging cranky children, and dancing to his own beat. Meanwhile, I'm scowling my way toward the coffeepot and groping for a mug. And this is not just an early morning thing. When we visit Walt Disney World (a happy bonus of being local residents), he is whistling and ready to close the park. I am melting down by noon. Every time.

The good news is, I'm learning to be aware of when I need to make an adjustment toward joy. I've come to realize that I am the CMO—Chief Mood Officer—in our home. When I am annoyed and uptight, the whole family is on edge. If I am stressed, everyone is stressed. Sure, the kids' fighting or lack of sleep or something else may be at the root of my mood. But I've discovered it doesn't really help to figure out who caused what. I just need to break the cycle.

As CMOs of the house, we moms have some amazing superpowers. We carry delight and joy in our very fingertips and eyes. Our children crave our love, touch, and approval. They want to know we see them and we love them even when things are going downhill. If the mood in the house is tense, we can assess if it's because we ourselves are too busy, too stressed, too critical, or too tired. Often bringing in joy is as simple as scooping up a little one to give him a heartfelt hug or smile and word of affirmation. You can almost see the life come right back into his heart. As adults we get the same feeling of affirmation from our heavenly Father during our prayer time and time in His Word.

Have you seen true joy up close and personal? I will never forget the morning I saw true joy, and I wanted it. I had recently moved to Orlando from Atlanta, and this new friend came over for a play date. Nikki's two little kids were running around in the playroom with my girls. Ever attempted a mom conversation while kids run wild? I was basically watching and waiting to pounce on mine for a "bad friend" infraction or "don't embarrass your mother" moment. I don't think I had looked my girls in the eyeballs that entire morning. I was probably making sure my house looked abnormally perfect for my guests.

60 Ways to Bring Out the Giggles

4

Daddy Disco.
Play an old '80s tune, and pull out your craziest dance moves for the kids.

And then I noticed Nikki do something incredible. Her daughter Madison came running from across the room, *so* excited to show her something. Nikki didn't rudely interrupt me, and she didn't do an arm block or wave her daughter away to play. She simply took a few seconds and literally beamed ear to ear with her child. She got face to face with her, grabbed her cheeks, and heard that angel's precious story. It froze me.

Here's what I saw: pure joy, simply because that child belonged to her and loved being in her presence. Don't you think that's how our Father probably looks at us? Isn't that the face we want our kids to remember?

Ten Ways to Break a Bad-Mood Cycle

Here are a few ways I've found to give our household an infusion of joy.

1. **Tickle Attack.** Chase down someone and tickle until belly laughter erupts.
2. **Play Hide-and-Seek.** This old-school game works every time.
3. **Cuddle Up and Read a Book.** Take turns with a timer if you have multiple kids.
4. **Funny-Face Contest.** Have them start behind a wall and jump out.
5. **Dance Party.** Burn a CD of your go-to tunes to have on call for when moods start to spiral down.
6. **Encourage Someone.** Loving on others takes the focus off us and replaces crankiness with compassion.
7. **Change Scenes.** We often jump in the car for a sweet-tea run for Mom or walk to a playground to get our smiles going.
8. **Indoor Tag.** Let them chase you around the house. (Consider earplugs for high squealing.)
9. **Play.** Crazy concept, but making time to play with them or style a crazy hairdo for them is a surefire joy starter.
10. **Listen.** I take turns asking them questions from silly to insightful. (What made you happy? What would you do if…?)

I have to be brutally honest here. Sometimes the lack of joy in our home is only because I am dealing with a trial. If my jeans don't fit or I'm behind on a deadline, things are tense. That might just be life, but I

5

Mom's Soprano Solo.

Sing the menu for the evening in an operatic style.

don't believe it is acceptable to carry on this way. I want to recognize when my own issues are trickling into the moods in the home and the way I handle my kids. They are just playing loudly or giggling like kids, and now suddenly they are in trouble because I cannot find an e-mail or I lost something again.

Some days I need sufficient caffeine to break the bad-mood cycle. Sometimes I need to get honest about my busyness and create room to breathe and do only the things God actually called me to do. Sometimes I need that text from a friend reminding me to get in my Bible. Time with God always sets my mind straight on my many blessings and brings me back to a biblical perspective. Sometimes I just need to smile even in the midst of a hard day. Often, I need to literally count my blessings.

Joy Begins in Our Hearts

Have you ever met a kid who is always joyful? One who always smiles when told to set the table and who pleasantly heads to bed at the first gentle reminder? Me neither. Whether driven by hunger, the need for a nap, or the desperate desire to find the right color socks right now, most kids can go from mellow to meltdown in three seconds or less. Just seeing a sibling get attention or approval can set off a chain reaction of jealousy and whining and decidedly unjoyful behavior. So we have to brace ourselves for reality. I have been claiming "she's teething" for about seven years every time my oldest acts ugly in public.

Please note that you do not have to change who you are or try to alter the God-given personalities of your children in order to pursue the virtue of joy. Some of us are naturally melancholy rather than exploding extroverts. Your personality and your child's were designed by the Creator of the universe in His image. But God also designed us to experience the deep joy that comes when we make the choice to rest in the assurance of His love. We need to know, and we need to teach our kids, that God is in control, no matter the circumstances. Security fuels joy, not bubbly personalities.

For adults, this means choosing joy when there still isn't a raise or promotion, or when your best friend lost weight again and you gained, or when you face incredible loss. For our children, it's choosing joy when your best friend is in the other class or your sister gets a big recognition or you didn't make that team.

This may sound simple, but living with a greater joy takes practice. For me, the practice includes praying, spending time in God's Word, and writing down His blessings in my prayer journal. I have to text with a friend and eventually get grounded in truth and biblical perspective. Sometimes I simply flip through family photos to remind myself of all that I have and shift my focus off all that I don't have. For my kids, I have to lead by example. I have to walk them through the tiny frustrations to life's biggest trials and keep pointing them back to our greater joy. I have to help them giggle after a quick fall and celebrate a friend with a card when the other person won that race or award they had hoped for.

I'm not suggesting we become plastic people with no negative emotions. It's good to show our kids how to work through sadness or disappointment. The danger is when trials come and we continue complaining

Catch Phrases for **Joy**

The language we speak in our home helps underscore the truths our children will carry with them through life. In each chapter, I'll include some catch phrases you can weave into everyday conversation to reinforce the virtue you are focusing on with your family. Warning: if used often enough, these might be the very phrases your kids will repeat when they are old. Don't you sometimes catch yourself quoting your parents? "My mom always said..." Here are some catch phrases to redirect attitudes and highlight the virtue of joy.

- Joy is a choice every day.

- Jesus Christ is the source of our joy.

- I have delight in my soul because I am a child of God.

- Let's praise Him in all things, even when things don't go our way.

- Great friends do not steal joy; they celebrate others (even when life doesn't go our way).

- Your happy heart shows on your cheerful face.

- Joy spreads through our family and then out into our community.

- Yes, that is disappointing, but _____ (insert something to thank God for).

or arguing or whining or waiting in a season of anger. Instead we want to take the opportunity to choose joy.

Life is busy and life is hard, but I will fight the pull to be dragged down by my moods. I will pray the source of my joy carries me through and reminds me to praise Him in all things. I can do this; you can do this. If we try one month of infusing joy in the hearts of our kids and in each room of our home, cheerful faces are headed our way.

Teaching Joy

A happy heart makes the face cheerful, but heartache crushes the spirit. *Proverbs 15:13*

Virtue Definition for Memorization

Joy: choosing to praise God in all things

Read in *The Jesus Storybook Bible*

"Get ready!" page 170. God's people return from being slaves, based on Ezra 7; Nehemiah 8–10; Malachi 1; 3–4. (For family Bible time, consider adding joy with a surprise location—an inside picnic, in a fantastic fort, or over a campfire eating s'mores.)

Questions for Discussion

- Is joy a choice or a feeling?
- Does joy have to do with your circumstances or surroundings?

- What is the ultimate source of joy?
- Share a story of a friend or family that has chosen joy during tough times.
- Name a joyful family that embodies this virtue.
- How could we share Christ through joy in the next month?
- Have you ever had someone steal your joy? How did that feel?
- Is there a special event coming up we can help celebrate for a friend?
- What happens when you don't feel joyful?
- What happens as a result of our joy?
- When do we have the most joy as a family?
- What is one thing we can do together as a family this month to choose joy?

Pray

Use our memory verse to pray over and with your family. For example,

Lord, I pray we will be a family of happy hearts. We want our faces to become cheerful because of the choices we make with our hearts. We want our joy to shine so that people know our joy comes from knowing and trusting You. Thank You for how much You do for our family; it gives us so much joy. We love You. Amen.

Activity: Joy Field Journal

For this month, you are a family of scientists. Your field journal has one goal: research joyful people. At school, at church, at the grocery store, and definitely at home. Your goal is to examine others closely to identify joy.

Supplies

- ☐ journals (one per family member)—make some at home, or pick any small notebooks or journals
- ☐ costumes—anything from detective gear to a scientist jacket and goggles; get geared up to closely examine those with joy

How This Works

You are on the lookout for joyful people.

- *Count them.* How many friends at school were joyful just because? Or during a tough day, they still had a smile? What about teachers? What about mom and dad? Did you see anyone at the grocery store? the park? How about the mail carrier?

- *Draw them.* Field journalists sketch their subjects. Draw these people, and add labels or conversation balloons. Did they have smiles? Or was there something else? Did they use hugs to show their joy? Did they speak words of encouragement to alert you that they were joyful? Did they sing songs? What did they look like? act like? Draw details in your journal to help you remember.

- *Analyze them.* Make notes and questions. Are they happy or joyful? Is joy contagious? Did you see it spread at school or at home from one person to another?

This is a family project. Ideally, family members will each keep their Joy Field Journal with them all month long so they can make notes as they notice joy happening around them. Then set aside a regular time to share and discuss your observations, perhaps every Sunday evening around the dinner table.

Additional Discussion Questions

1. How does a person's joy affect others around her?
2. Do all joyful people look and act alike?
3. Did you notice a friend who is facing a trial but is choosing joy?
4. How can you tell if someone is joyful by our definition of "choosing to praise God in all things"?
5. Were some of these people just happy people? Were you able to find some who had joy because of the Lord? What is the difference?

Further Instructions

Mom and Dad, be sure to immediately point out and affirm joy in your own kids on the spot! It can certainly come up in the weekly discussions, but immediate positive reinforcement is necessary for helping your children recognize the virtue of joy.

Don't forget to write the virtue definition and memory verse in your journal!

Optional Activities

PLAN one family activity or outing that makes your family joyful when you are together. Let each family member share some ideas.

READ & DISCUSS scriptures on joy: Romans 15:13; Galatians 5:22–23; James 1:2–3; 1 Peter 1:8–9.

ENCOURAGE Write a letter to one family or person who embodies this virtue.

Love

Letting Concern for Others Guide Our Behavior

Memory Verse for the Month

We love because he first loved us. *1 John 4:19*

I am not sure there is anything more pitiful than a giant cup of frozen yogurt dumped on the sidewalk, especially when the victim of such tragic loss is a five-year-old Shirley Temple look-alike. My daughter Larson's best friend, Harper, had worked so hard filling her cup with just the right blend of yogurt and toppings. You know, the combination that would make us adults gag on first bite: gummy worms and sprinkles topped with something in the neon-sugar family. After perfecting their deadly treats, my girls and Harper and her sister were headed down the sidewalk to find a bench. (I know, yogurt on the move is a bad idea.) Then the sweet curly headed angel flipped her cup into the air—

Feather Test.
Who can sit still
the longest with
a feather being
rubbed under
his nose or chin?

gasp—and it plopped onto the pretty sidewalk of St. Simons Island.

She didn't cry, but her puckered-out bottom lip almost made me cry. I ran to her with my cup of yogurt, and all the girls immediately started picking toppings from their yogurt and placing them in her cup. You could practically see her heart filling back up, and the girls clearly felt delighted to help someone they love.

Love is a complex topic and extremely hard to define, but you sure do know it when you bump into it. One of my teaching pastors at Summit Church, Jim Keller, said he bumped into love right after his heart surgery. He was helpless as he watched his wife bend down to put on his socks and shoes and then tie them every day.

I bumped into love the other day when a scene in the play we were watching terrified Larson and she buried her head in my chest. Her big sister noticed her fear and reached over to rub her back and kiss her head. My heart swelled up.

My friend Melissa bumped into love when she witnessed a selfless moment in her home: her little girl, Emma Grace, saw her dad doing yard work in the Florida heat and on her own took him a cold drink.

Sometimes, I feel the truest sense of love after I've been snippy with my kids and then get down on their level and, with all my being, beg for their forgiveness. And with all their being, they say, "Yes, Mom. I forgive you." And they wrap those arms so tightly around me.

Seeing our kids express genuine love is a heartwarming experience.

Yet all too often that me-centeredness of our children rears its ugly head. Just this morning one of my children was crying huge tears because the other one was getting *more* at the dollar store. How about loving and supporting your sister who earned her rewards? And what about when one child hurts the other and the culprit's first reaction is to blame? This one makes me go nuts. I want the first reaction to come from love: "Are you all right?"

The fact is, we are all born self-absorbed. Children need to be taught to fight against their natural tendencies, and we can accomplish this through role modeling and practice. As my mom said, "Training a heart to be sensitive to others, it *can* become a natural instinct." By taking advantage of everyday teachable moments, we can teach our kids that putting others before themselves is exactly what Christ has done for us.

Biblical Love Is Our Goal

As I mentioned earlier, *love* is incredibly difficult to define. For our purposes here, we're going to skip past romantic love to focus on biblical love and how we want to share it with our kids. Here are a handful of truths that help shape our understanding of biblical love:

- Love is why our faith works and why we serve one another (Galatians 5:6, 14).
- Love binds us together (Colossians 2:2).
- Love gives others joy (Philemon 1:7).

As we've heard so many times, love is an action, not a feeling. I have certainly experienced moments when I choose to love so that my feelings might follow. However, don't we all yearn for sincere and genuine love to be at the core of our children's hearts, guiding their behavior? When Ella reached over and consoled Larson during that play, it blew me away. I wasn't forcing her. It came from a true moment of love for her sister. That is the goal.

Here is our definition for this virtue:

Love: caring for others, expecting nothing in return

Note the two key elements of this definition: (1) love is focused on others, and (2) love is given without preconditions. I desire a home where love is more than just words or a feeling; it cares and keeps no records, much like the love described by Paul:

> Love is patient, love is kind. It does not envy, it does not boast,
> it is not proud. It does not dishonor others, it is not self-seeking,
> it is not easily angered, it keeps no record of wrongs. Love does
> not delight in evil but rejoices with the truth. It always protects,
> always trusts, always hopes, always perseveres. (1 Corinthians
> 13:4–7)

I want our love to overflow from the love we have received from Christ. This kind of love reflects our heavenly Father and aligns with what Jesus said are to be our highest priorities:

> Jesus replied: " 'Love the Lord your God with all your heart and
> with all your soul and with all your mind.' This is the first and
> greatest commandment. And the second is like it: 'Love your
> neighbor as yourself.' All the Law and the Prophets hang on these
> two commandments." (Matthew 22:37–40)

It seems clear from these words that loving God and loving others aren't optional for the family that wants to follow Christ. Will others recognize our faith by what we say? by how big a cross we hang above the front door? by how many times we take our children to church?

Jesus said, "By this everyone will know that you are my disciples, if you love one another" (John 13:35). Knowing that, I want our family's genuine love for others to shine so bright that it can only point to our Savior.

Love the Ones You're With

One of the surprising gifts of motherhood is amnesia. Have you lost as much short- and long-term memory as I have? Where did we go for vacation two years ago? I have no idea. What did we eat for lunch yesterday? Not a clue. I want you to know I was not always a ditz. I had it together before my amazing children came along. I could run multiple marketing campaigns in my brain, not one list needed. Now I keep about fourteen legal pads scattered around my home, and I still cannot get it straight. I am the mom whose kid is wearing the wrong uniform or who is begging a friend to give my child a ride because I triple-booked myself.

7

60 Ways to Bring Out the Giggles

Tongue Twisters. Look up popular tongue twisters, and challenge each other at the dinner table to say them faster and faster.

So if I actually remember something, you can be sure it carried a wallop of impact. About five years ago, my friend Kristine said something about love that struck me deeply and has stayed with me ever since. In fact, it is the reason behind the "Love 'Em Up" activity in this chapter that originated from a blog community effort. Kristine and I were discussing how to teach her two boys and my two girls to love others and share and be kind.

It was like a record-screeching moment when Kristine said, "I am laser focused on brotherly love right now. If they can work to love each other well, they can pretty much love anyone."

Isn't that the truth! Love is learned by practicing it on those we spend the most time with, those who are most likely to push our buttons and draw out our me-centered responses.

Kristine's point led me to write a song for my girls, called "Sisterly Love." Here's a sample of the lyrics:

Sisterly love. Sisterly love.
We say kind things and we love each other.
Sisterly love. Sisterly love.
We share our toys and play with each other.

Sisterly love. Sisterly love.
We have a lot of hair and that's from our mother.
Sisterly love. Sisterly love.
We have the same nose and that's from our father.

It goes on and on—and so do the giggles.

When life gets heated, Ron and I will launch into this song, loudly. It's become one of our favorite tools for dissolving tension between our girls.

Kristine's comment reminded me that our family members see the very best and worst of us. If we can teach our kiddos to treat each other with genuine, unconditional love, we set them on a path to love teachers, friends, and teammates well.

I have noticed that this month's activity, Love 'Em Up, often has some side benefits. While the main goal is teaching kids how to love their siblings and their parents in unique ways, this assignment has grown my girls' confidence in their abilities. When we throw out an idea and then give our children the time and space to rise to the task, beautiful things happen. They are far more capable then we often give them credit for.

I asked my girls one morning during our own Love 'Em Up season to simply "make Mom's job easier at some point today." I honestly forgot about it by lunch. And then I was hunting for some important papers, and my sheepish sweet Larson said, "Mom, your papers are under your desk. I put them there because I cleaned your desk for you." I almost kissed her nose off her face right then and there. She had voluntarily completed a task I never would have dreamed up.

8

Puppet Show. Grab or make a puppet, and take turns putting on a show.

60 Ways to Bring Out the Giggles

However, love isn't always sweet and easy. This goes for relationships inside our home and out. Loving the most difficult of friends, even loving our enemies, is a critical part of biblical love (Luke 6:27–36). Sometimes, we need to lead our kids in praying for their enemies or in choosing to do a kind act for someone who hurt them. Love sometimes means holding back our words when we've been hurt. This is tough to model, even in adult relationships, but our children are watching us. Can you imagine how our choice to set aside anger and choose love sets the stage for them as adults? Learning how to love in difficult situations as they grow up will help them navigate complex relationships later in life. This month's activity offers many opportunities to live out this idea of loving the ones you are with, practicing how to care for others and expect nothing in return.

Always and Forever

God's unconditional love is hard for me to grasp, even as an adult. I don't necessarily deserve His love, but I am loved. I don't have to perform a certain set of tasks, yet I am loved and there is grace. I want to model this kind of love in our home. I try to find ways to remind my girls they don't have to perform for my love or their dad's. They are loved simply because they belong to us. They can mess up and still come back home. We often say, "Do you know why I love you? Because you are MINE!"—just to remind them they don't have to do anything or be anything to earn our love.

Ella and I share the common bond of tender hearts. We both cannot sleep if things aren't right between us. She is devastated if she is in trouble or feels she has disappointed us. So when she was about three, we came up with our motto: Always and Forever. I explained to her that, just as God loves us always and forever, nothing could ever separate her from our love. We have turned this into a nightly reminder.

It never hurts to remind our kids that the God of the universe loves them always and forever. And so do we. We remind our girls often of this promise:

> For I am convinced that neither death nor life, neither angels nor
> demons, neither the present nor the future, nor any powers,
> neither height nor depth, nor anything else in all creation, will be
> able to separate us from the love of God that is in Christ Jesus our
> Lord. (Romans 8:38–39)

Catch Phrases for **Love**

As discussions or challenges come up during this month, try using some of these catch phrases to reinforce the virtue of love.

- God's love for us is everlasting, just like my love for you.

- Loving someone may not always be convenient for you.

- Loving others feels so great in your heart, doesn't it?

- Did you know loving others makes God smile—and your parents too?

- Loving your sister/brother isn't always easy, but it is always important.

- Loving someone doesn't mean we get the credit or proper response. It means we do our part well.

- When you are caring for another person, you are choosing to love.

- I saw you notice a need and take care of it. Way to show your love! Thank you.

- What a creative way to show your sister you love her! Look at her smile. Way to go!

- I've seen you grow so much this month. You are making so many choices to love your family. Wow.

We also discuss this powerful description of how much God loves them:

> And I pray that you, being rooted and established in love, may
> have power, together with all the Lord's holy people, to grasp
> how wide and long and high and deep is the love of Christ.
> (Ephesians 3:17–18)

We want our girls to know that Christ first loved us—not because we earned it or deserved it, but because He is love. All the love we show to others comes from the overflow of His love for us.

Becoming a Student of Our Children

Among my adult friends, the hurt kid deep inside occasionally bubbles up and they tearfully say, "I know I was loved as a child, but I didn't feel loved." I know exactly what they mean. Ron can sweep the floor and rub

60 Ways to Bring Out the Giggles

9

Duck, Duck, Goose. Have all family members join in for this old-school fun.

my back for three weeks, but I don't feel loved until he speaks to me with encouraging words. That's because words of affirmation are my love language, as described in Gary Chapman's powerful book *The Five Love Languages*. I love that Gary came out with an edition specifically for parents: *The Five Love Languages of Children.*

One of our most important jobs as parents is to be students of our children. Sometimes we hit walls in our family relationships because we haven't fully cracked the code of how our kid feels love. This month we are going to be learning just as much as teaching. As we try different methods of showing love, we'll be watching to see which ones really answer each child's emotional need. We want to be sure that, on an ongoing basis, we are caring and loving in a way that speaks directly to the other person's heart. A special dessert treat may make one child feel extremely loved, while another comes alive when you take time for a date night. When I walk into the school to pick up Ella rather than waiting for her in the carpool line, she lights up with love. Ella's love language is quality time. When I set aside my phone and snuggle together with Larson, she feels

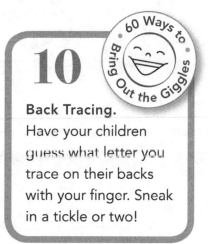

10

Back Tracing.
Have your children guess what letter you trace on their backs with your finger. Sneak in a tickle or two!

60 Ways to Bring Out the Giggles

loved. Her language is physical touch. I am learning my girls. And while they may change with age and seasons, their core love languages should be revealed and remain consistent over time.

I can think of few more rewarding goals than becoming students of our children—and teaching them to naturally do the same for others, starting with the ones right in front of them each day. As we discover for ourselves what touches the hearts of our family members, we can help our kids grasp how best to care for others as well. Larson might not view making Ella's bed as an act of love until she sees the relief in her sister's eyes at having one less chore on her list and more playtime after school.

I pray that when we feel the urge to change our children, we'll instead fight to learn them. And as we learn them through the years to come, we will be able to love them—and help them love others—better and better.

Teaching *Love*

We love because he first loved us. *1 John 4:19*

Love: caring for others, expecting nothing in return

"The forgiving prince," page 76. The story of Joseph and his brothers, based on Genesis 37–46.

- Do you feel our family is sensitive to the needs of others around us, both inside our home and out?
- What are some ways you best feel loved?
- What do you think makes each member of our family feel uniquely loved?
- What ideas popped into your head for showing love to others in our family?

- What could you add to your routine that would surprise another person and make that individual feel super special this month?
- Are you loved only when you are doing the right thing? Why do mom and dad love you?

Pray

Dear Lord, we want to be a family that overflows with Your love. We want to love others because You first loved us. Will You give us new eyes to see our sisters, brothers, and parents as precious gifts? Remind us how to care for them and never expect a thing in return. We know You created our family to show Your love. Lord, help us to learn the best way to love each other and all those You place in our path. Help us do it so well that we bring You glory. We love You. Amen.

Activity: Love 'Em Up

The best place to help our kids practice loving others is in our homes. Family members can be tough to love, but I believe if we can tackle these humans first, we'll be ready to love up a school-teacher, a classmate, or a friend. So this month we're going to focus on loving our families well through random acts of kindness right inside the walls of our homes.

Imagine a home where siblings serve each other out of love. Yes, Mom, you have to intentionally surprise and love on the most challenging kid. And, Dad, you're playing too. Sisters who want to pull out strands of each other's hair are about to get really close. From sibling to sibling, mom to dad, child to parent, we're going to practice the art of loving each other well.

Let's love 'em up!

Supplies

This activity can be executed with items already in the house—existing note cards, food from the pantry—or with a simple investment of your time. But if your budget allows, you can have a lot of fun surprising one another with special little gifts throughout the month.

How This Works

Love 'Em Up is easy to implement. The mission is simple. Fill the house and your family's hearts with L-O-V-E!

February is a great month to try this activity since we're already focused on love and stores are stocked with valentine products that tie nicely into these ideas. But any month is a perfect time to practice love.

All month long, everyone in the family will look for ways to serve and love on others—sometimes without the other person's even knowing! The possibilities for easy yet thoughtful tasks range from painting a sister's toenails to making a brother's bed. You can assign names or simply let everyone love on everyone else. I'm confident that this month's task can remain in the family budget using household items, but if you won the lottery and feel like a hot-air-balloon ride would tell your kids you love them as far as the eye can see, go for it.

Love 'Em Up: Sibling to Sibling Surprises

- Do one of her chores.
- Make his bed.
- Fold her laundry.
- Help him with homework.
- Give her a manicure or pedicure.
- Clean his cleats.
- Dust or vacuum her room.
- Clean his side of the bathroom.
- Organize her closet.
- Sort his toys.
- Leave a note on the mirror in lipstick or eyeliner saying why you love her.
- Slip a note in his Bible, journal, or book bag.
- Notice her or encourage him at school in front of friends.
- Post-it note attack her room, stating all the reasons she's great.
- Support him with extra love by encouraging him at his hobby or sport.
- Prepare a favorite snack or treat for her, just because.
- Let him borrow your favorite toy or clothing item.
- Give a sincere hug with a genuine "I love you, sis/bro."
- Write ten reasons you love being your sibling's brother/sister.

Love 'Em Up: Child to Parent Surprises

- Make your parents' bed.
- Leave flowers by mom's nightstand.
- Have coffee ready for mom in the morning.
- Make breakfast for dad.
- Leave a note for mom in her Bible or journal.

- Leave a note for mom or dad in their work bag.
- Go to mom or dad's work and sneak a treat in their car.
- Put mom's favorite candy in her purse.
- Help mom with chores.
- Decorate the door with notes to welcome dad home.
- Organize a bathroom or closet to lighten mom's load.
- Clean the garage for dad.
- Create a sidewalk-chalk greeting for dad.

Love 'Em Up: Parent to Child Surprises

- Make heart shapes with anything! Pancakes, strawberries, waffles, toast, sandwiches, cinnamon rolls, pizza, and more. Anything says "love" when it's shaped like a heart and you spent extra time on it.
- Add a special topping. A squirt of whipped cream, a cherry on top, sprinkles. Any little extra yes when we normally say no lights up those faces and communicates love.
- Decorate with hearts. Post heart-shaped notes that specifically describe what you love about your child. Hang a strand of hearts from your child's bed, doorway, or mirror.

Love 'Em Up: Miscellaneous Ideas

- Let each person go around the table and simply say "Mom, I love your…" or "Dad, I love you because…" or "Larson, I love when you…" After each person says something about each member of the family in order, let everyone jump in at random with expressions of love.
- Parents, send each other an e-mail or text saying why you love each other.

- Parents, write an old-fashioned love letter and leave it in your spouse's Bible or journal.
- Parents, let your kids see affection as you offer a sweet greeting or good-bye at the door.
- Parents, let your kids play while you two spend time catching up *in front of them.* Knowing mom and dad love each other assures kids that their home life is safe and secure.

Optional Activities

PLAN a family night themed around love, from music to décor to setting. Let the kids plan it based on all the things the parents love to eat and experience. They can choose an after-meal activity, such as a family walk, a game night, or soccer in the park.

READ & DISCUSS 1 Corinthians 13:4–8; Galatians 5:6, 14; Colossians 2:2; 3:14; 1 John 4:7–8.

ENCOURAGE Who do you know that loves really well? Maybe a specific person came to mind as you read the verses. Encourage that person and thank him in writing for loving you so well.

3

Forgiveness

Discover the Freedom That Comes Only Through Grace

Memory Verse for the Month

Be kind and compassionate to one another, forgiving each other, just as in Christ God forgave you. *Ephesians 4:32*

I'm that mom. Love me, hate me, join me, or laugh at me. You just need to know the DeFeo girls are totally getting dolled up for Easter. Even if our pastors make a joke about it every year and encourage us to wear our jeans and relax. I've been dressing baby dolls and dreaming of dressing real baby dolls since I was a little girl myself. So when we actually have somewhere to go outside of Costco and Target, there will be big bows and big fluffy dresses. I haven't busted out any white gloves or bonnets, but never say never. That said, please hear me: if you are the mom wearing jeans on Easter, I love you and we can sit together to worship the King of kings, knowing He doesn't give a rip what we are wearing. We are clothed in the grace and the forgiveness of Jesus.

11 Movie Time. Have each person act out a scene from a favorite movie.

Although I love the frills and fun of Easter, I know it means so much more than egg hunts, festive activities, and patent leather. Every time I arrive at church on Easter morning, the weight of the day takes my breath away. I sit and surrender to the pure truth that I am forgiven. The choices I made in college. The way I treated my husband yesterday. The one hundred days I missed time in God's Word. All forgiven because Jesus endured torture for me and for my kids.

The same is true for you and your family. You are loved; you are forgiven.

Forgiveness is a gift from our heavenly Father. And the lessons we teach our children about the virtue of forgiveness are all rooted in that incredible gift. If they learn the art of forgiveness and move beyond the basic apologizing technique, what will that mean for their hearts? What will it mean for their relationships? their stories of faith? their authenticity as followers of Christ? How might they handle bigger, heavier issues of anger and resentment if they learn how to forgive freely now? What if our children realized the freedom that comes with moving on versus insisting on their way and being right?

The ability to understand and live out forgiveness will shape the future fabric of your family. If you are like me, you long for your children to grow into lifelong friends with one another and, when the time comes, to bring their own babies home to you frequently. If you come from a family that didn't practice forgiveness, you know how those wounds hurt—and you want to give your kids a different legacy.

What a gift we will have given to our children if they leave our homes knowing how to set aside anger, bitterness, and resentment and instead embrace freedom, love, and forgiveness. This is a tall order. Certainly, forgiveness and fun don't seem to fit together at first glance. However, forgiveness clears a path to joy and giggles. When we walk with our families toward grace—through giving and receiving forgiveness—our steps are lighter.

It takes great humility, a virtue we'll explore further in chapter 10, to admit not only when we are wrong but also when we've been hurt. Ultimately, genuine forgiveness requires the work of Christ in the hearts of our children. Let's prepare the soil of their hearts for His harvest of grace. We do that by living out the forgiveness we've received from Jesus.

In my home we've had plenty of opportunities to practice. I find it a daily challenge to love my family well and keep my cool. Do you, too, feel as if you mess up more often than you get things right? I find myself praying for the hard days to be erased from my girls' memories. I am so thankful that God's mercies are new every morning, strengthening me to forgive my kids and forgive myself.

I pray that you and I will aspire to create the safest homes on the block. Homes full of love, joy, and laughter, where our kids are free to return at any age to resolve issues, share their hearts, admit a wrong, or even ask us to realize how we've wounded them. Homes where we thank them for their courage, where we don't snap in defense during confrontation, where we hear their hearts and take responsibility for our part in any conflict. Homes where we never expect perfection but commit to continued growth, where we end difficult conversations with a hug, and where we always point one another back to the only perfect way: the love of Jesus.

Teaching the Cross to Kids of All Ages

As Easter reminds us each year, the supreme example of forgiveness is given to us through Jesus's death on the cross. But how do we begin to instill this powerful truth in the sensitive hearts and minds of young children?

When my girls were just toddlers, we hadn't really discussed death. I felt uncomfortable launching into a conversation about nails and blood and someone hanging on a cross.

What I adore about North Point Ministries (the church we attended in Atlanta when the girls were younger) is their ability to break down basic biblical truth into age-appropriate teaching. I have always gleaned so much wisdom from their approach and resources. I also lean heavily on the resources and creative thinking of Orange (The reThink Group), an organization led by brilliant leaders helping churches and families raise tiny disciples.

60 Ways to Bring Out the Giggles

12 Capture the Flag. Create a family flag, then hide it in the house. First to capture the flag wins something.

With their strategies in mind, I realized we didn't need to overwhelm our preschoolers with heavy theological principles. Yes, our faith hangs on the story of the Cross and the Resurrection, but that doesn't mean my three-year-old needs to understand the full import of Ash Wednesday or the Lenten season. We've always tried to put big words into terms they can understand, then grow their understanding as they mature.

When my girls were little, I loved to read them the popular board book *What Is Easter?* by Michelle Medlock Adams. I would also remind them, as we headed to church in our finest, that Easter Sunday has nothing to do with a bunny and everything to do with Jesus and His love for us. And following in my mom's footsteps, I've always included something in their Easter baskets to grow their faith, from a new devotional to a new Bible or VeggieTales DVD.

This year, we hosted a Good Friday play date by inviting several of my daughters' friends and their moms to mark the special day with us. We loved it so much that I believe this will be an annual event. We organized several activities for the kids to help reinforce the meaning of the Crucifixion and Easter. We ended the time together with a project inspired by my friend Sara Easley: stuffing plastic eggs with extra change and loving notes. As they left, each family took eggs to deliver to people in need within our community.

As Ella and Larson have grown older and started asking more questions, our game plan has been to keep talking and explaining as best we can what happened at the Cross. We try to be clear about what we know and honest about what we don't know yet. Just recently, Larson expressed some confusion about the Trinity. That's a tough topic for adults, let alone a five-year-old. I reached out to my good friend Kylie for a way to handle biblical topics that are beyond a child's current understanding. I love her answer: "In our home, we often say this phrase to our kids, based on the promise in Psalm 139:17–18: 'If God's knowledge outnumbers all the grains of sand, then my understanding is like one grain.'" Another great response might be, "That's a good question. I don't know. Let's pray on that tonight and talk some more tomorrow."

For school-age tweens and teens, I'd suggest that you ask questions to see how much they already know. Let them direct the conversation. Make your dinner table a safe place to discuss and debate how God's forgiveness, love, and grace changed history and make a difference in our lives.

Teaching Forgiveness to Kids of All Ages

Of course, forgiveness is not relevant only at Easter. We frequently pray together and thank God aloud for His forgiveness so the message starts taking root at an early age. So what exactly is forgiveness in biblical terms? It is an act of obedience to God to forgive as He first forgave us.

This is the definition for this month's virtue:

Forgiveness: erasing a wrong with love

As my husband said, "It's a heart issue." He's actually great at this. While I'm still steaming over a disagreement, he comes in humbly with a sincere apology for his part and seeks forgiveness. He's always understood it matters very little who is right or wrong, who was worse or first; it's about coming forward with a loving spirit ready to erase the wrong with love.

The thing about forgiveness is that we find it easier to offer it to others when we recognize how often we need it ourselves. Learning repentance—recognizing and admitting our own wrong behavior—is an integral aspect of learning forgiveness.

We can begin the critical task of encouraging our children to take responsibility when they wrong someone just as early as they can talk. "I'm sorry for hitting you. Will you forgive me?" And we model forgiveness by our response: "Yes, I forgive you," followed by a warm hug. We can also model repentance in our relationships with our kids. "I'm sorry, buddy, for getting angry. Mommy was wrong for losing her temper. Will you forgive me?" Looking these little ones in the eyeballs and seeking their forgiveness can be a powerful experience for both parties. Especially because some of us find it hard to admit our imperfections.

With some kids, it's a downright battle. If you have a strong-willed child, I wish I could pray with you right now. Simply trying to get that child to say "I'm sorry" might take an entire month. Trust me. I've been there. I also remember when both my children finally, around age five, began apologizing or asking others for forgiveness without any prompting from me. I melted. After years of the "repeat after me" drill, their own hearts were nudging them to erase a wrong with love! I always celebrate when this happens. Big deal in our home. No, they don't come running back with a repentant spirit every time, but more often than not, if I give them a minute to think about what just happened, they'll come out with

60 Ways to Bring Out the Giggles

13

Swim Indoors. Fill up a bathtub, slip into your swimsuits, and pretend you're at the beach!

the proper response and attitude. I'm so grateful for this progress.

The hope, of course, is to help our children move beyond the automatic responses of "I'm sorry" and "I forgive you." Forgiveness is so much more than saying the right words. We can say "I'm sorry" with fury still raging in our voices and hearts. Such responses don't mend relationships or smooth over resentments. I believe God intended much more for our families than verbal forgiveness; He wants us to respond in light of the compassionate forgiveness we've received from Him. As our memory verse reminds us, the goal is to "be kind and compassionate to one another, forgiving each other, just as in Christ God forgave you" (Ephesians 4:32).

Essential components of forgiveness are compassion and empathy, so we need to help our kids put themselves in another person's situation or imagine what someone felt like. In our home it might sound like this: "Wow, Mom got really frustrated. I bet that sometimes you feel sad and hurt when I raise my voice. I don't want you to feel sad, because your heart is important to me. I'm so sorry I hurt your feelings." Or we might try engaging them more in the apology conversation instead of forcing a robotic response. I might ask, "How did you feel when your sister did that?" and then suggest the other sibling incorporate that into the apology.

14

Movie Night. Make a pallet on the floor and pop some popcorn. Have all the family snuggle together, phones off.

My friend Emily and her family had an opportunity to practice forgiveness recently when her son was being bullied by a classmate at school. After weeks of discussing it as a family, Emily was impressed to share with her son the words of Jesus in Matthew 5:44: "But I tell you, love your enemies and pray for those who persecute you." Frankly, she didn't want to go this route. She was still angry at how her son was being treated. But praying for their enemy is exactly what this family did.

After some time, Emily was thrilled to hear that not only was the situation much better but her son was happy to include the bully in his group of friends. She watched his heart turn from resentment to love for a friend. How powerful prayer and forgiveness are to change the hearts of kids and adults alike.

As believers and parents, we have a responsibility to teach our kids that forgiveness is actually a bridge to personal freedom. It's about so much more than accepting someone's apology. It's about building relationships. It's about nurturing healthy hearts.

To give and receive forgiveness shows humility. It requires that we admit we are not perfect and we need a Savior. We can choose whether or not to handle life's mess-ups biblically, remembering that little ears and eyes and hearts are watching closely. I pray you and I will have the courage to be open about our mistakes and about the process of restoring relationships. Let's show our kids the peace that comes when we are quick to forgive others and quick to ask for forgiveness.

I used to believe forgiveness was mostly about setting the other person free, but I found that offering it brings healing and freedom for me. Lewis B. Smedes wrote in his book *Forgive and Forget,* "When you release the wrongdoer from the wrong, you cut a malignant tumor out of your inner life. You set a prisoner free, but you discover that the real prisoner was yourself."[4] Holding on to anger, bitterness, and resentment is not healthy.

Have you been surprised to hear your kids harboring anger, bitterness, and resentment at early ages? I have! Our bedtime conversations typically reveal such topics as I pose open-ended questions like these: "How's your heart? What was the high point of your day? the low point? What made you happy or sad?" I have often found that the real truth of their hearts peeks out in the darkness of snuggle time. Or on the way to school, when I ask how I can pray for their day, the answer often reveals situations that weigh heavily on their hearts.

Our children's hurts are sometimes hard for us mama bears to hear. If you're like me, it can be hard to listen without pouncing with a solution or a plan to confront the wrongdoer. At times I've pounced too quickly and only embarrassed us both. I'd do better to help them learn to handle it on their own. My dear friend Bobbie Wolgemuth told me recently, "My job as a mother is not to remove all my children's problems, but to teach them to handle them biblically."

During the quiet moments when their hearts are open, we can lead our children through critical moments of growth. We can show them that forgiveness starts with them, no matter who initiated the problem. We can point them to truths in God's Word that will give them wisdom for today's problem and tomorrow's.

Practice Forgiveness Daily

If your house is like mine, someone is typically apologizing or crying by 7:30 a.m. Which means that, like it or not, we basically have a daily school ground for learning this virtue. Rather than despairing, let's seize those opportunities to practice daily. Eventually, we and our children will develop hearts of compassion, hearts that choose to forgive because we are forgiven by our Savior.

Since we want our children to practice sincere forgiveness, not only saying the right words but truly meaning them from their hearts, to follow are a few helpful tips I've discovered about teaching this virtue in the multitude of everyday opportunities that arise in our homes.

Help Them Own Their Responsibility

When our kids say "I'm sorry," they are basically just owning up to a mistake, right? Are their hearts truly remorseful for what they did? The forgiveness process leads them to healing and acknowledges motives of the heart. When they are little, we need to help them, perhaps by encouraging them to "repeat after me": "I am sorry. I was wrong for _____. Will you forgive me?" Eventually they'll be ready to do it on their own.

Help them resist talking about anything other than their own part in the problem. If they start pointing fingers or bringing up excuses, help them see that's not part of the apology equation. We are only concerned with taking responsibility for our own part.

I also like to encourage my girls to follow up an apology with some expression of love—a sincere hug, kiss, or note.

Try a Delayed Response

Have you noticed your child suffers from selective memory? When you promise your son a trip to get ice cream on Tuesday, he applies a laser-sharp focus. He knows the date and time you said it—and he's not about to forget. But if he has some math homework or has lost his Wii privileges for three days, such facts often seem to slip his mind. He has absolutely no recollection of these details.

I bring this up because we parents often think we have to immediately demand our children take action when an apology is due or they'll somehow forget. Don't let their "memory fake out" get you.

Yes, it's usually most effective to point out an issue when it's fresh. But that doesn't mean we have to demand they find an immediate resolution. Sometimes I like to say, "I didn't like the way you two treated each other. There will be a consequence for that later. Meanwhile, I need you to think of a proper way to apologize to each other." And I give them a chance to get their hearts engaged on their own. I can force an immediate robotic "I'm sorry," or I can wait to see if a heartfelt note appears saying "I was wrong to take your doll. Will you forgive me? I love you XOXO."

Choose Less Dictating, More Questions

One of my favorite mom moments happened recently on the way to school. The day had started out horrific, with both girls being really ugly to each other. And I was steaming. The tension was thick. For once I didn't yell in my frustration. I didn't proclaim a consequence. I simply let them know how disappointed I was and then asked, "How do you think that makes God feel?" I gave their hearts a chance to process my question. About a minute later, my sweet Larson piped up, "Mom, how do you spell 'Do you forgive me'?" And with tears in my eyes, I spelled every letter so she could write her sister a note.

I'm convinced that if we do less dictating, they will begin to respond from a beautiful place: Christ in them. Let's give them a chance to do the right thing.

Let It Be Between Them and God

I typically don't like my kids to keep secrets from me. Surprises, like conspiring with dad to make mom breakfast in bed, are absolutely fine. But while we generally discourage secrets, I do think a journal is a safe and private place for them to write out their hearts to their heavenly Father. I want them to know He's their best friend and they can go to Him anytime, with or without me. If they don't know how to pray about an issue specifically, or if they are hurt and need to let something go or ask forgiveness—and they aren't ready to share it with me—I'm absolutely okay with my kids taking that to God in their own journals.

Focus on Restoring Relationships

I want my girls to know that once forgiveness has been offered, it is finished. The matter is closed. Jesus, mom, or dad is not going to hang things from the past over their heads. I want them to feel the freedom of letting things go, of moving on in a restored relationship after they've received or offered forgiveness.

Sometimes, however, after the words have been spoken, someone is still mad. My sister-in-law gave me a great idea for this. After minor squabbles, I put my girls literally nose to nose and have them repeat loving statements (often dictated by me): "You are my sister. You are my best friend. I am sorry I hurt you. Will you forgive me? I love you. Let's have a great day together. I love having fun together. My heart feels better. Does yours? I love you sooooo much." They can't stand there for long and not start giggling. And when giggling comes back in our home, I typically know hearts are mended.

As they age, I will give them space and time to find their own way forward, but I will still help them work toward the critical step of fully restoring that relationship.

Catch Phrases for Forgiveness

- What's your piece in this problem? Where do you need to take responsibility?

- I was wrong when...

- Our choices affect others.

- Everyone makes mistakes. Should we hold on to anger or be quick to forgive?

- When we choose to restore a relationship instead of keeping track of wrongs, we show great love.

- How can we right a wrong today?

- I know you love your sister (friend, teacher, and so on); how can you show that love?

- We want to be the first to offer forgiveness, because God forgave us.

Celebrate Progress

This morning, Ella accidentally smacked Larson with her booster seat. Often her embarrassment at hurting her sister prompts Ella to get mad. This time, however, she said, "Larson, are you okay? I'm sorry." I quickly jumped on the opportunity to praise her for showing compassion to others.

As we see our kids make great choices in seeking or giving forgiveness, let's praise them. Celebrate with them the way Jesus is at work in their hearts.

Gifts of Forgiveness

Can I confess something? Sometimes I'm the one most in need of a reminder about the virtue of forgiveness. When I lose my patience with my children, it's so easy to think, *They made me do that! They caused me to sin and get mad.* I know, I know. They are children and I am the adult. I need to take responsibility for my own part.

I don't want to leave my girls with spirits broken, believing they have let me down and they are not in good standing. And I don't want to stay there myself in my relationship with God, as if my heavenly Father has lost patience with my lack of self-control and so is going to withhold His forgiveness until I can get my act together.

Do you know the feeling? Can you remember feeling you had let your parents down and they hadn't forgiven you? Or they said they had forgiven you, but you know they hadn't forgotten?

Here's the truth about God's forgiveness: "As far as the east is from the west, so far has he removed our transgressions from us" (Psalm 103:12).

I am so grateful the Lord is letting this truth sink deep in my very own heart this morning. As far as the east is from the west, so far has He removed my sins and mistakes as a mother. If my creator does this for me, why can't I do this for my very own children? Or my husband?

My little one was hurt the other night. I kept speaking into her heart and trying to get her to look me in the eyes. As I reassured her of my love, she finally received the message and melted into my arms.

15

60 Ways to Bring Out the Giggles

Design a Fort. Build a fort with sheets and dining chairs.

Here's the challenge of forgiveness for you and me: Do not let go. Do not give up. Do not ever stop pursuing those young hearts. God has never let go of me and you, and He never will.

I pray for grace to fill my heart each day. I want to have compassion and kindness just like my Savior. I want ours to be a home full of forgiveness and unconditional love, a place where my children believe grace is real because they've experienced it.

But I also want my kids to know there is only one Person who is perfect, who will never let them down. Mom and dad will surely try to be perfect; we will try to love unconditionally. But we are going to mess up. Often.

We were never meant to be Jesus to our kids; we were meant to show them Jesus. That's a vastly different role and set of expectations.

You and I aren't here to get it right or get it perfect. We are here to keep pointing our children back to Jesus. To help them understand why they need Him. Why He made them. Why He forgave them and how absolutely breathtaking that truth is.

The most wonderful part is that with the Cross came forgiveness for all. It's a beautiful story worth telling over and over again. And if your family is as imperfect as ours, you'll have plenty of chances to talk about redemption and forgiveness and grace and love. The ending is always the same. God loves. God saves. God forgives.

Teaching Forgiveness

Memory Verse for the Month

Be kind and compassionate to one another, forgiving each other, just as in Christ God forgave you. *Ephesians 4:32*

Virtue Definition for Memorization

Forgiveness: erasing a wrong with love

Read in *The Jesus Storybook Bible*

"The sun stops shining," page 302. The story of the Crucifixion based on Matthew 27; Mark 15; Luke 23; and John 19.

Questions for Discussion

- Are you forgiven by God sometimes or always?
- Tell me about a time when you were really hurt and no one apologized.
- What does God have to do with forgiveness? Do you know the story of the Cross?

- Should we keep count of or hold on to our sins? What about the sins of others? Does God keep count?
- Is there anyone you are angry toward? Are you willing to ask God to take away that anger?
- Why is it important that we forgive others first? even our enemies?
- What does forgiveness do for the hearts of both parties?

Pray

Lord, we are in awe of the Cross and what it means for our family. We cannot believe the sacrifice You made for our lives and our sins. Please search our hearts. Let us be quick to forgive those who make us angry. Help us be the first to show love when we are hurt. Let us also be quick to ask for forgiveness when we have wronged someone else. We want the truth of Your amazing story to flow through our lives. Thank You for the Cross. Thank You for Your forgiveness. Amen.

Activity: Our Family Cross

This activity is suggested for right before Easter but can work anytime of the year. The idea is to illustrate the powerful sacrifice that Jesus made on the cross and bring the word *forgiveness* to life for your children.

Supplies

- [ ] two sticks to make a cross (finding these is part of the activity)
- [ ] several nails and a hammer
- [ ] pot filled with soil or rocks, large and heavy enough to hold cross upright
- [ ] scrap paper
- [ ] tacks or small nails
- [ ] flowers or greenery, either silk or real (keep this hidden from the kids)

How This Works

As a family, go on an adventure in your own yard or a local park to find just the right sticks to make a cross for your home. The bigger the better (you'll find an example at courtneydefeo.com). At home an adult will nail together the two sticks and stand the cross upright in the pot. Place it prominently in a family gathering place for the week leading up to Easter or for the night before.

As a family, brainstorm a list of sins or things we do that are displeasing to God—things like not sharing, being disrespectful, talking back, or yelling—then note each on a separate scrap of paper. Avoid getting personal ("when X sister does this"). Use tacks or nails to attach those sins to the cross. I suggest that parents go first in humility, listing sins and nailing them to the cross. Then have the kids add their ideas. You could also ask them to put up a description of any situation where they are holding on to anger. Once finished, take a photo.

After your children go to sleep that night, take down the papers and run them through the shredder or toss them in the fire. However you choose to do it, be sure they are destroyed. You and your spouse may want to pray over these sins as you destroy them, asking that forgiveness will become real in your children's hearts and that they will discover the freedom of letting God erase these things from their hearts.

Place flowers or greenery all around the cross. You could also add a new piece of paper in the shape of a heart, listing on it the name of each family member. When they wake up Easter morning for breakfast, your children will find a beautiful surprise waiting! He has risen! And all our sins are forgiven, completely gone. That is what Jesus did on the cross; He erased all wrong with love.

Optional Activities

PLAN a trip to the library to bring home Easter books focused on the Passover or the Resurrection.

READ & DISCUSS Psalm 103:12; Proverbs 15:1; Isaiah 1:18; Matthew 28:6–10; 1 Corinthians 15:57; Ephesians 4:26; 1 Peter 4:8.

ENCOURAGE Sometimes hearts change more easily through writing. Encourage your children to keep a journal or write a note to God or the other person involved in a painful situation, explaining why it hurts or why they are sorry for their part in the problem.

4

Faith

Planting Seeds of Trust for a Lifetime of Spiritual Growth

Memory Verse for the Month

I have been crucified with Christ and I no longer live, but Christ lives in me. The life I now live in the body, I live by faith in the Son of God, who loved me and gave himself for me. *Galatians 2:20*

Let me tell you about a little boy with big faith. Marshall is the firstborn child of my dear friend Ashley. He has eyes that make you melt on the spot and a gigantic heart.

After struggling with infertility a couple of years, Ashley and her husband, Jon, proceeded with the adoption process for their second child. Marshall prayed,

"God, please give us twins." And his parents laughed. Do you know what happened? About the time their adoption referral came through, Ashley unexpectedly got pregnant. They now have two girls, just six months apart. One day, Marshall put it all together and said to his mom, "God answered my prayers about twins."

Oh, the wonder of childlike faith!

Our own faith can be strengthened as we watch our kids grow in their understanding of God's love. Some of my most beautiful moments with God have come from experiencing the faith of my children. When my girls receive an answer to prayer or grasp a new truth, it is truly amazing. These faith-growing moments aren't because of my efforts, but because of God working through His Word, a song, or a teacher. I'm thankful just to be present to celebrate or talk it through or expand upon what their hearts are processing. And often my heart needs to hear the very same lesson they received that day.

Is your faith as big as your child's? Are you overwhelmed by the weight of what you want your kids to know? Do you feel like you've made a mess of your efforts to teach spiritual truth? Do you worry they are too old and it's too late?

16 Bible Charades. Act out the most common Bible stories.

In talking with hundreds of moms on this very topic, I've noticed one consistent theme: as moms, the depth of our desire to bring faith to life in our homes is matched only by the depth of our insecurity. Every mom worries she is dropping the ball. Every mom carries spiritual guilt. Upon hearing a child recite his Scripture verse perfectly, all the other moms in the room want to bang their heads on a brick wall and declare themselves a failure.

Why are we so stressed about this? If we fail at homework, our struggling student can get tutoring help. If we fail at planning meals, we know they'll eventually eat something. If we fail at instilling faith, however, we fear their eternity is at risk.

I have great news for you. It is not too late! Your child is not too old to be guided toward a life of faith. You have not missed the opportunity, and you have not ruined it. You can make the decision today to trust Christ and walk a path to bring your family closer to God.

I have more great news. It's not all up to you! You have an extraordinary opportunity to set the tone in your home and lead your children into a daily experience of faith. You can partner with your church in teaching truth. You can sing praise songs and pray every day. However, we have no control over our children's decisions to pursue faith or to flee. God is the One who moves in their hearts. And God is enough.

Faith as We Go

My oldest, Ella, was just a baby when my mentor gave me the giant gift of freedom wrapped in the form of a Scripture verse.

I desperately wanted to raise my children to love God and make wise choices. I wanted to do all the right things. I had visions of our family sitting around the table calmly having devotions. But as I faced the reality of life and our family dynamics, my hopes had started slinking away in discouragement. Then Regina shared this verse and this truth with my mentor group:

> Write these commandments that I've given you today on your
> hearts. Get them inside of you and then get them inside your
> children. Talk about them wherever you are, sitting at home or
> walking in the street; talk about them from the time you get up

in the morning to when you fall into bed at night. Tie them on your hands and foreheads as a reminder; inscribe them on the doorposts of your homes and on your city gates. (Deuteronomy 6:6–9, MSG)

As my mind absorbed those words, I felt shackles breaking off, a lifting away of the parenting mandate I had placed on my own heart. I had thought I needed to follow certain guidelines or a formula to successfully pass faith on to my family. But in reality the Bible outlines a simple approach: I am to do life with my family and talk about faith and Jesus wherever we are, in the midst of real life. When my kids are scared at night, faith comes up. When we are on a hike and the beauty of creation grabs our breath, you'd better believe we are talking about our God. When we hear our children comparing themselves with one another, we use those moments to speak of how each of us is made uniquely for a purpose.

I pray this passage lifts a weight for you too. Your kids don't want a lecture on what you know; they want to experience who you know. They want to know your heart, and they want to know how God might be relevant in their daily lives. They want to know that your belief in the one and only God is certain and that it directs every aspect of your being: "I have been crucified with Christ and I no longer live, but Christ lives in me. The life I now live in the body, I live by faith in the Son of God, who loved me and gave himself for me" (Galatians 2:20).

Essentially, faith is about inviting our kids to the party. It is thrilling to watch God work, and I cannot wait to share with my girls when it happens. One time, an old friend kept coming to mind. After the third nudge, I decided to reach out to her. She was blown away and said it had to be God because she was having the worst day as a mom in all her years of parenting. She asked if I would pray for her. This moment reinforced my faith. That result could have been enough, but I also wanted to use this as a memorable teaching opportunity for the girls. I let them know that our passing thoughts, many times, are not random. It's important to be alert to how God might want to work through us.

Our families want to see us trust God not only in the struggles but also in the triumphs. Let's show them Jesus. They need to know Him more than they need to hear us. I believe it's the experience *together* that helps guide their faith journey.

Let's start with a definition we can all memorize and understand:

Faith: knowing, loving, and following Jesus

Your child's faith is the heartbeat of this book and truthfully my motivation behind it all. This is the one that matters the most. I'm so thankful my parents were intentional so that I would experience "knowing, loving, and following Jesus." So let's consider the opportunities we have to be similarly intentional about creating an environment where faith can thrive.

Knowing Jesus

Wondering if and when my girls would "accept Christ" or "become a Christian" honestly gave me the cold sweats. I also thought that once that was accomplished I could take off to Italy knowing my job as a parent was done. Now I realize getting them to trust in Him is just the beginning. I yearn for children who want to follow Him and know the depth of His love. I am eager to watch them experience their part in His big story and the thrill that comes with being a part of something eternal.

I had a nudge in my heart to keep waiting for Ella. She was five and hearing all the right things. When her best friend made the decision to trust in Jesus Christ, to proclaim He was her personal Savior and ask Him into her heart, Ella naturally wanted to go next. But I chose not to follow through on her comments, partly because I wanted her decision to come from her own desire to know Christ, not from peer pressure, and partly out of my own fear and insecurities (oh, Court of little faith!). I worried I might say the wrong thing or mess it up somehow. My fear came from a place of personal performance, which I can admit is silly and sad.

60 Ways to Bring Out the Giggles

17

Family Ice-Skating. Grab some paper plates and go ice-skating in the kitchen.

One night we were reviewing some memory verses, and we got to John 6:47: "Very truly I tell you, the one who believes has eternal life." She asked about eternal life. And I just told her right from my heart what I deeply believed was true. I didn't scare her into a declaration of faith. I told her great news that we get to spend a lifetime with God when we choose to believe in and follow Jesus. And she so sweetly asked if we could pray together. Her face and heart lit up. She shared her news with Daddy. Soon after, on her sixth birthday, we gave her a charm with the word *believe* to mark that special year of her life.

I'm convinced one of the greatest gifts we can give our kids in the journey of faith is the freedom to explore at their own pace. The freedom to experience Him personally and take ownership over the process. A mandated faith is a faith headed for fizzle. This means it is more than okay if your child hasn't shown an interest by age five. While some kids will announce their belief with a bold proclamation, for others salvation is a process of years of growing and trusting. Just keep reminding yourself that only God, not you, can change your child's heart: "Salvation comes from the LORD" (Jonah 2:9).

If you are not sure where your kids are with this decision, please do not panic.* Remember who made them. God! Who is working every day in pursuit of their hearts? God! Do not pressure them.

Pray for them. And prayerfully consider finding some partners in this journey. Who will you lock arms with to influence your child's heart for God?

Partners in Discipling

Think back over your life. What had the most significant influence on your journey of faith: books, places, people, things, or events? I would guess that it was the people! Some for the worst and most for the very best.

I am no idiot. I know the days are numbered until my sweet little girls begin tuning me out. My word carries weight with them now, but before long they will care far more about what others say and think. That's why Ron and I want to ensure we lock arms with others who care deeply about the hearts of our children, to create a team of incredible men and women who are devoted to raising our kids to be authentic disciples of Christ.

We think long and carefully about environments in which our kids spend time. We care deeply where they go to church. I'll be bold enough to say that we care more about their experience than ours, but thankfully many churches excel at programs for both adults and kids. We care about the families with whom they visit most regularly. We care what teachers

---

* If you are reading this and cannot honestly say you know Jesus Christ personally, the very best gift you can give to your children is making that decision to believe and follow Him. Your life will never be the same. Find one friend and tell her this desire. If you don't have someone, I'd love to be the one. E-mail me at courtneydefeocom@gmail.com. It would be my absolute honor to lead you to your heavenly Father.

and leaders are pouring into their character. I have already made a list of women who might mentor my girls as teens and asked a few of them to begin speaking into my girls' lives and affirming them now. I trust these women like sisters to walk with my girls and be there for them over a lifetime.

From camp counselors to baby-sitters to friends who spend the night, countless voices may influence what our children think about their faith. Let's do what we can to be sure these relationships are healthy and an accurate picture of a God who loves them deeply. I realize we can't surround them with a protective bubble, but surely we can do more than send them out into the world and cross our fingers, hoping someone will speak truth into their hearts. God places children in families so they will be protected and provided for in many ways, certainly in the area of faith.

Bible Time

We simply cannot know, love, and follow Jesus without reading the Bible! That is where we learn about His promises, His love for us, how to handle conflict, how to love others, how to love God, and more. The Bible is our guide for life. It's a source of encouragement and comfort for our family, not just a book of rules.

Making the Bible a consistent focus of family life might mean reading Bible stories before bed or talking about creation on a walk. As children grow to know more about God's interactions with His people and how Jesus responded when He walked on this earth, they will begin to insert their lives into those stories. They'll gradually grasp what it means to be in relationship with Him and to watch for His hand at work in their lives. At our house we absolutely love *The Jesus Storybook Bible,* and my friends raising young boys love *The Action Bible.*

Along with reading the Bible and talking about its truths, we wanted our children to memorize scripture. In doing so, they absorb truths that can guide them for all their lives.

As a mother of two little ones, I realized early on I needed an authority other than myself to point my girls to. One day in particular was a nightmare of toddler antics coupled with exhaustion. I kept yelling "No!" and "Because Mom said so!" Eventually, both the girls and I were crying. And I knew there had to be a better way.

There are reasons you cannot smack each other with a doll. There are reasons you cannot speak like that to Mom. There are reasons you are to be kind, always.

"Because Mom said so" just doesn't hold much weight after the first 409 times in a day. So I began searching for easy Scripture verses for us to memorize. I liked the idea I had seen others use: tying scripture memorization to the alphabet.

18

Kiss Attack.
Kiss each child one hundred times quickly.

60 Ways to Bring Out the Giggles

But I really wanted a teaching tool that would stay out in my home where we'd see it all the time, something that would both decorate and teach. As I discussed this with my friends, my idea for a personal resource developed into a new product.

I worked for a long time with my mentor, Regina, to pick just the right mix of verses. Then I launched ABC Scripture Cards online in October 2011 and eventually sold the concept to Magnolia Lane, which has expanded sales to retailers all over the United States (while allowing me to keep family life my priority). We continue to use these alphabetical memory verse cards regularly in our home, and now when my girls confront a problem, I have something better for them than just Mom's wisdom.

For example, Ella recently came home and told me, "A friend was mean to me."

"What did you say back?" I asked.

"Nothing."

"Well done, Ella," I encouraged her. "What's the K verse? That's right:

Ten Fun Ways to Bring Faith to Life

1. Simply ask "How's your heart?" often! And when they answer, invite God into their story for comfort, encouragement, or wisdom.

2. Have new readers read *Jesus Calling: 365 Devotions for Kids* out loud to the family. All are learning, plus a little one is practicing his reading.

3. Make dinnertime WOW time. Go around the table and share a praise, a reason to say "Wow." Where did you see God show up this week? Or today?

4. Memorize scripture to silly tunes and cheers. Let kids record on your phone's video or voice recorder to practice.

5. For teeny tiny ones, sing "Jesus Loves Me" and other songs packed with truth to them every night at bedtime.

6. Pick a verse to pray all year long for each child. Trace their hand, and write the verse on the cutout of their hand. Laminate it and place it in your Bible. Date and save!

'Keep your tongue from evil.' We never want to say anything rude back, even when someone hurts us."

It was working! We had truth in our hearts and a way to parent using God's Word.

Memorizing Bible verses is meant to be not a dry discipline but an interactive experience in which we show our kids that the words they're committing to memory are "alive and active" (Hebrews 4:12). This

7. Make a carpool challenge! On the way to school, give kids one easy idea for living out their faith that day. For example, let a friend go first in the lunch line.

8. Play "What Would You Do If...?" My kids love to be heard, and I love to hear their answers. Pose questions like these: What would you do if you learned a friend had never heard of God? What would you do if someone said God isn't real? What would you do if one friend was unkind to another friend?

9. Mark the occasion. Whether it's a birthday, back-to-school night, or major milestone, it's important to show kids that every event that matters to them matters to God too. Take a moment to write a heartfelt letter, pray together, or arm your child with an appropriate scripture.

10. Play praise music. We clean up to praise music. We drive to school with praise music. We do dance parties to praise music. What a fun way to let God's truth sink straight into a child's memory and heart.

practice lays a foundation in their hearts that sets them up for a lifetime of comfort, security, and guidance. That's because God's Word never returns empty (Isaiah 55:11).

Praise and Worship

This one is a home run. I cannot tell you how often praise music has absolutely saved our day. I will have started out yelling, and then a praise song will transform my attitude, prompting me to stop and beg for forgiveness before they leave my arms for school. I have been driving with tears, feeling like a failure as a mom, only to hear my girls boldly singing from the back seat "Oh, how He loves us!" at the top of their lungs. I have been cleaning the house, feeling run down and overtired, when a Scripture verse we set to a funny tune spills out of Larson's cute mouth while she plays. "I am the way, the truth, and the life!" (John 14:6, NKJV).

Music reminds me of the Disney Fast Pass. It has a way of racing past the nonsense of the day and getting straight to the good stuff. You almost forget about the fight and the bad attitude that was just flowing through the house because you are immediately transformed by the words and the sounds. Your foot taps and you get your twirl on. God's Word and His promises come to life through praise and worship music. It's something any parent can use today to redirect a family's attention toward faith.

60 Ways to Bring Out the Giggles

19

Play Telephone. Whisper a message, then send it down the line of family members; see if the first message is the same as the last one.

Thankfully, musicians including Casey Darnell,[5] Yancy, Chris Tomlin, TobyMac, and Jamie Grace have made praise and worship a family affair. You almost don't even realize the truths you are absorbing, and then an incredible line pops into your head right when you need it.

We clean the house to these tunes, we save a disastrous road trip with these songs, we have raging dance parties (often jumping from coffee tables) to irresistible choruses, and we do a lot of air guitar and pliés. Join us, if you dare.

Prayer Life

Another way we follow Jesus in our family is through our prayer life. I want prayer to be more than something we say before meals. I want it to be a natural reaction to life's ups and downs. I don't want to reserve prayer for times of fear or worry; instead I desire to live a life nourished by proactive prayer that continually trusts in God.

Just the other day, Ron brought the girls to my room and had us all hold hands as he prayed for my upcoming speaking trip and for the words I would use, that God would use me to help the moms know Jesus better and be encouraged. I was deeply touched by the incredible example of trust in God he showed our girls.

We pray with our girls over their biggest trials and tiniest troubles. We do not overreact when they get silly and pray for a fork or a frog. We've noticed that the more they practice, the more natural it becomes and the deeper their understanding sinks of what it means to talk with God.

As you pray with your children, I encourage you to celebrate when prayers are answered. When my Larson learned she did not have to take her reflux medicine ever again—an answer to four years of prayer—that was a moment for celebration, marked with jumps and squeals. We called everyone we knew. My brother's church rejoiced along with us and moved her to their "healed" list—and she got it. She knew God had heard her prayers. Together we bowed our heads and gave Him great thanks.

The Cost of Faith

Do you ever hear something like this at your house? "But, Mom! They can watch that show! They called me a baby because I don't." "But, Mom! Why can't we go to that movie?" "But, Mom! My friends are allowed to say that word." "But, Mom! But, MOM!"

Whether you're a seven-year-old or a grown adult, following Christ can cause tension in relationships. Every family does not do it the same. Jesus Himself said there would be a cost for following Him. You might even be ridiculed for the way your faith guides your personal choices.

I try not to base our parenting decisions on what other people are doing. We are responsible for our family. I do care about how our kids respond to others. Raising kids who follow Jesus means teaching humility and grace, along with discernment between right and wrong, so that choosing God's good ways doesn't lead them to be self-righteous and judgmental. The challenge is to carefully equip our children to navigate their roles as followers of Christ in ways that draw people to Him rather than steering them away.

Although I love Jesus, I find it sad that I struggle to love some of His people whose intentions may be pure or biblically right, but whose approach repels the very people God wants us to love. I believe this is a major part of teaching our kids to follow Jesus: showing them how to hold tight to truth while leading with grace and humility.

There will be certain activities and trends in which our family will not participate because of our faith. At other times our faith will compel us to walk right by the side of someone on the outskirts of life. I want to follow in the footsteps of Jesus, who walked with the tax collectors and outsiders who needed His love. My girls have gone with me to eat lunch with the homeless and hear their stories. They have driven with me to shelters to see how we could help. It will always be my intention to *be* the church more than *talk* about church.

Following Jesus is often messy. However, that is why our kids have their heavenly Father and parents to guide them in the path of love and grace.

So let's stand strong and never forget they are following us. Are we following Jesus? Is the stress of our lives and every event tossing us around like waves? Or are we rooted and grounded by our faith? Do our children see us earnestly seek and trust God's will? Are we chasing things of this

Catch Phrases for **Faith**

- We believe in God even though we can't feel Him, touch Him, or see Him.
- Faith is knowing, loving, and following Jesus.
- God created you and made you so uniquely special.
- You can tell God anything, anytime!
- Our family trusts God with our lives.
- Is that pleasing to God?
- You have such amazing gifts from your creator, and I can't wait to see you impact others for His glory.

world and dragging the kids along? Or are we on a pursuit of eternal matters, showing them the ultimate fulfillment of following Christ?

My friend Sandra Stanley often prayed the following words with her kids when they were young: "Heavenly Father, give us the wisdom to know what's right and the courage to do what's right, no matter what people think."[6] I love how this prayer points our children to God for daily guidance.

Do Your Best—and Leave the Rest to God

Bringing faith to life in our homes is a great privilege, but we don't have to have it all figured out in order to see God move in the hearts of our kids. He has got this. Our role is to simply teach them what we know and to continue learning and sharing more day by day.

You can make a difference even if you're only one second ahead of your children in your own journey to know Jesus Christ better. Your fear and your uncertainty can show them God's grace and mercy. Your mistakes can teach them forgiveness. Your strengths can shine a spotlight on God's blessings and gifts. Your daily ordinary tasks can become extraordinary opportunities to reach the hearts of your children. They will see a sunset through

60 Ways to
Bring Out the Giggles

20

Accent Scripture Memory. Go around the dinner table and say the same verse in different accents—one person might do his best British accent, another might speak with a southern accent, and so on.

the lens of the Creator with your prompting. They will see friends as gifts to handle with care because of your hard work.

My prayer is for your children and mine to experience faith in a way that etches God's goodness in the very depths of their souls. Rather than giving them a narrow version of faith that emphasizes fear and consequences and "don't do this," let's help them experience firsthand the truth that the God of the universe loves and forgives and accepts them. Let's make our homes safe for questions, places of comfort and security where parents live out a faith overflowing with God's love and grace.

And when moments of doubt and spiritual guilt settle in, don't forget your heavenly Father loves those precious souls even more than you do. He wants to equip you for this journey, if only you will turn to Him for wisdom, discernment, guidance, comfort, and peace. So grab hold of Him, and never let go.

Teaching *Faith*

Memory Verse for the Month

I have been crucified with Christ and I no longer live, but Christ lives in me. The life I now live in the body, I live by faith in the Son of God, who loved me and gave himself for me. *Galatians 2:20*

Virtue Definition for Memorization

Faith: knowing, loving, and following Jesus

Read in *The Jesus Storybook Bible*

"The beginning: a perfect home," page 18. The Song of Creation, based on Genesis 1–2.

Questions for Discussion

- What is faith?
- Who is God? Jesus?
- Is God a friend? a father? What makes you say that?
- Why does God matter in our lives today?
- What has Jesus done for our family?

- How can we glorify God in our daily lives?
- What's your favorite thing God created?
- As a family, how can we love God? know God? follow God?

Pray

Dear Lord, these children are Yours. You created them to play a part in Your huge story. Show me how to guide them and shape them for that part. Give me discernment, strength, wisdom, and peace. Use our family to show others Your great name. I thank You for those in our family who started this legacy of faith. Let us honor that decision in the way we follow You each day. Let us make decisions that will inspire future generations of our family. We love You so much, and we want our faith to shine bright because of how much we love Your people—just as You do. Amen.

Activity: Our Heritage of Faith

What is the best book to reference as pure evidence of God's faithfulness and work on this earth? The Bible! What if our kids had another book to grab that contains stories of families they know? Names and places they have experienced in their own lifetimes? What if their dad wrote a journal entry describing a time God showed up and met him in a struggle? What if their mom recorded a story of when she trusted God and He answered her prayer?

Imagine your family's testimonies becoming your children's bedtime stories. From prayers answered to lives transformed, once upon a time the God of the universe showed up and touched the lives of your very family members.

Let's capture your family's heritage of faith in a journal, a storybook that will grow through generations to come.

Supplies

☐ one large, sturdy journal

How This Works

Set aside a special family time at least once a week throughout this month to start a record of your household's faith journey, as individuals and as a family. This journal would also be a great place to note special family milestones, such as salvation decisions, baptism or dedications, mission trips or service activities.

Get things rolling by posing one or more of the following questions to each family member and recording the answers:

- How do you know God is for real?
- When did you meet Him for the first time?
- Can you describe a time you knew He loved you?
- How have you seen God working in our family?
- When have you heard from Him clearly?
- Name a time you trusted your Savior above all else.

Your little ones could draw pictures to illustrate

- what they love most about God
- His best creation

- some of His promises from the Bible
- some of your prayer requests

This book could be a priceless gift passed on from generation to generation, especially if you make such conversations part of a family tradition. At your next extended-family gathering, your kids could interview their grandparents and ask similar questions.

If this is daunting or scary based on your family history or the lack of a faith heritage, don't worry about looking backward; just begin right where you are. Your family's heritage of faith starts today, with your story. What an incredible decision you are making for future generations.

Optional Activities

PLAN a night outside or picnic to tell stories or brainstorm what you want to put in your journal.

READ & DISCUSS Romans 5:1; 10:17; Galatians 3:26; Hebrews 11:1.

ENCOURAGE Write letters to three family members to thank them for making positive decisions that continue to impact your family.

5

Patience

Some Things Are Worth the Wait

Memory Verse for the Month

But if we hope for what we do not yet have, we wait for it patiently. *Romans 8:25*

Now that you are a parent, do you often cry at the Publix Super Markets commercials? Or at a random dad at the park enjoying his kids? Please tell me it's not just me. One of my favorite dads (and a fellow crier) is the super-talented songwriter and singer Casey Darnell. We became pals recently and have shared several teary moments talking about our kids and God's love.

When he told me the following story in my kitchen

(and tears were flowing), I just knew it had to go in this chapter. It's a beautiful illustration of the biblical virtue of patience.

Shortly after my daughter Ava turned three, an opportunity came up to go to Orlando later in the year with my wife's family. For us that meant one thing: *Disney World!*

We got real excited, as neither my wife nor I had been to the Magic Kingdom since we were children. So of course I told Ava where we were going in a few months and how amazing it was going to be. Ava was thrilled and jumped up and down and asked if we could go to the mall today!

"The mall?" I said. "Oh, Ava, sweet girl, we're not going to the Disney Store in the mall. We're going to the place where the princesses, whose dresses you wear daily, actually live and where Cinderella's castle is. And there are rides, and it's bigger than anything you can imagine!

"The Disney Store is sooooo much smaller, Ava, that you can actually fit our entire mall inside the Magic Kingdom. But we have to wait awhile before we can go."

I began to realize Ava had no idea of the reward her patience would bring, and she was totally content to settle for the Disney Store. So I tried again. "You see, Ava, the Magic Kingdom is a place that has been prepared just for *you*! It's a place filled with laughter and smiles and celebrating and memories we can make as a family and never forget. We have to wait awhile to go there, but trust me, it's going to be worth the wait!"

As we prepared for our trip, one friend gave me a tip that I'm forever grateful for: "Whatever you do, make sure you get around the corner first so you can see her face the first time she sees it!"

So when the day came, I did just that. With my camera in hand, I ran ahead and got set to capture it all.

Sure enough, she turned the corner and as her eyes widened, a smile lit her face that I will never forget.

No more waiting… No more confusion… We are at the *Magic Kingdom*!

When the day came to an end, I was carrying my little girl, fast asleep, out of the park. I began to be overwhelmed with new perspective. My mind flooded with emotions and memories. Memories of my dad carrying me out asleep and how that seemed like yesterday. Time had flown by, and now I was a husband and a father and experiencing life through new eyes. I couldn't help but think of what I had been trying to explain to Ava months earlier.

I began to hear the voice of a Father, saying the same thing to us all about our temporary home here on earth. Our willingness to settle rather than wait eagerly. We are content with the store in the mall when all the while He has so much more for us—if we'll only wait a little while, trust in Him, and believe Him when He says it will be worth it.

Life is full of hardship, and we run to so many things to help us get through it. If only we would instead hold on to His promises. Promises that His love endures and His strength is perfect in our weakness, that He is always with us and we were made for a purpose. Let's don't give up, but keep holding on to Him with hope.

The hope that, just as I told my three-year-old, it will all be worth the wait.

Casey's story beautifully describes the goal of this chapter: teaching our children patience because God's promises are worth the wait.

Patience is a tough virtue to practice, especially for children. However, it's critical to their lifelong walk with Christ. Learning to wait well translates into learning to trust well. If we can teach our kids to wait for dessert with happy hearts, maybe one day they can wait patiently for a spouse or the next house or the job they desperately need.

Reality Check

Telling young children to be patient is like telling a little boy to stop moving. We're asking them to go against their very nature. Our kids come out of the womb wanting everything *now!* And I'm not sure I am any different. If my Internet is down for more than twenty-two seconds, I begin huffing and puffing. If a car ahead of me doesn't move the second the light turns green, I'm ready to blow the horn. Am I the model of patience for my kids? Hardly.

In fact, I am probably one of the most impatient people in the world, which isn't great for a follower of Jesus. I get impatient with my kids, husband, and anyone or anything else that gets in the way of what I want. It's so embarrassing, and I confess to you this is a huge struggle.

My impatience bubbles to the surface in traffic, at the post office, in a carpool line, and pretty much all day. I just want to fly through life with zero waiting. So I essentially have daily opportunities to let my kids see how I will handle these moments. Will I honk? Will I be rude to the post-office lady because the line was long? Will I yell at my kids because I

60 Ways to Bring Out the Giggles

21

Hide-and-Seek.
Play a daytime game in the house—or play at nighttime using flashlights.

didn't prepare the night before and we are running late? Will I get frustrated because toddlers simply cannot get in and out of the car quickly or buckle in four seconds flat? Or will I breathe in and breathe out and pray?

I suspect that I'm not the only mom who didn't know she had an anger problem until kids came along. If you share my struggle, please lean in close. I wish I could hug you right now as I share this hope-filled truth I've finally learned: struggles are in our path so we recognize our need for God. When we are weak, He is strong. Whether you come from a long line of screamers or you've been shocked by the impatience erupting from your mouth, you don't have to carry a burden of shame. At this minute, you can wrap yourself in the grace and love and forgiveness from God above.

This parenting job is not designed for perfect people—but it is designed to create opportunities for God to work within us, to help us become more like Jesus every day. As we lean into Him for the strength we lack, He will develop patience in us. He may also use other people—a friend, a counselor, a pastor—to help us learn how to cope without resorting to anger or screaming.

If patience is a struggle for you, I invite you to seek God's heart, asking Him to nurture this virtue in your home and to show you what to do when you run short on peace. Throughout the Bible are reminders that God Himself is "compassionate and gracious, slow to anger, abounding in love" (Psalm 103:8). Who better to guide us in showing tenderness to our children?

Our kids feel love when we are patient with them. As 1 Corinthians 13:4 reminds us, "Love is patient." When I get impatient, I have to take a hard look at the root issue. Do I have too much on my plate? Am I getting enough rest? Am I expecting too much from my kids? Am I asking for help? Am I spending enough time with God to align my day and perspective with His priorities? Am I asking for wisdom, patience, and strength?

I ask God and I ask my husband to help me figure this out. I don't want our children to remember me as the snappy, angry mom. I want to show patience and love so they have a living role model for how they should treat their siblings, their parents, their future kids, and any other human.

Over time, I've taken little steps toward improvement, and I invite you to join me in moving forward. Let's kick impatience and anger far away this month. Together!

Opportunities Abound

The suggested month for focusing on this virtue is May. Most families are impatiently waiting for school to get out. If you're like me, you've lost all steam, drained of energy by all the homework, the papers, the laundry, the lunches. Attitudes are headed downhill fast. You kind of want to send them to school in flip-flops and sunglasses because you can almost taste the beach. Vacation is near!

Christmas is another ideal season to help our kids practice patience. *Is it here yet? When can we open that gift?* And what about waiting for a special date on the calendar like the birth of a sibling, a field trip, or a visit from a grandparent? Our schedules and lives are packed with opportunities to practice and improve how we wait. Are our homes packed with patient people?

Here's the definition we use at our house:

Patience: waiting with a happy heart

We've been practicing the virtue of patience almost ever since my girls learned to talk. They didn't have to know many words to express their impatience: "Are we there yet?" "When is my friend coming over?"

"Is my lunch ready?" "Mom, we have to go *now*." I learned quickly that yelling "Just be patient!" was getting us nowhere. Saying "Girls, we need to be patient. What does patience mean?" has helped. They recite (though usually with a frustrated face), "Waiting with a happy heart."

22

Staring Contest. Set two players face to face, and see who can stare the longest without breaking into a giggle, looking away, or talking.

It's not easy to walk away without complaining and wait until it's time for dinner or time for that craft. It's not easy to wait your turn or to be quiet while another family member is talking. Waiting is never easy, but those who learn to wait well are on their way to trusting God well. And that's the key to the "happy heart" part of our definition: we trust that God has good things planned for us even when the waiting isn't all that fun. Please understand, I'm not suggesting we pretend that waiting itself is full of joy. Sometimes it just plain stinks. But if our lives are centered on Jesus, we can find reasons to be happy even when life doesn't follow our ideal schedule. "If we hope for what we do not yet have, we wait for it patiently" (Romans 8:25).

So let's consider some practical tips on how to nurture the virtue of patience.

Avoid Unnecessary Waiting

Certainly we need to teach patience to our kids, no matter the age. However, not all situations are ideal for developing this virtue. And it's impractical to expect a two-year-old to sit silent and still in a chair at a restaurant for two hours while his parents linger in conversation. Smaller practice sessions at home will help children develop self-discipline, but expecting too much too soon leads to major anxiety for both parents and kids— and can ruin a nice, fun, family dinner.

I have learned the hard way that sometimes it's better to avoid circumstances that require more patience than our kids have at the ready. If your favorite restaurant has an hour-long wait, you might have to choose an alternative or get creative. Maybe order carry-out and make it a fun night at home. If your child has not yet learned to stay seated long enough for a full-blown trip to the grocery store, you may need to leave him home with the other parent until he has toned up those patience muscles.

Also, I proclaim from personal experience that 4 p.m. might be the worst time ever to run errands. At 9 a.m., young children can stay in carts and manage to be reasonably happy. By 4 p.m., they have used up every last shred of self-control and so has their mom. I might suggest you avoid asking your kids to wait for much of anything at that time of day. It's simply not the ideal classroom for cultivating this virtue in a joyful way, and any ill-advised efforts are likely to end in frustrated tears—for mom and child.

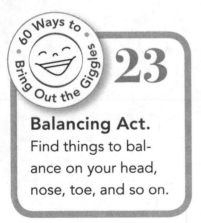

60 Ways to Bring Out the Giggles

23

Balancing Act.
Find things to balance on your head, nose, toe, and so on.

It might also be wise to avoid giving too much advance notice of upcoming activities to little ones who have no concept of time. Resist telling them about a vacation or a birthday party or something exciting, particularly if you have one that might ask every four minutes for the three months leading up to the event.

Improve Waiting

For those occasions when our kids do have to wait, I think it's a great idea to show them it doesn't have to be torture. When we as adults must wait for the next job or for a call back from a friend, do we cry and mope or stomp around? I hope not. We need to show them that a season of waiting can be productive and fun.

For preschoolers, you might keep handy an entertainment bag. I keep a bag hanging in the closet and ready for restaurant visits. It's packed with crayons, stickers, games, and other distractions to help us wait with happy hearts. Elementary age and older kids can pass the time productively with homework, scripture memory, and reading. Recently, mine were melting down at dinner, and I just started asking them questions. "What is your favorite meal?" "What would you do for a day if you could skip school?" They love to be heard.

To channel anticipation for upcoming big events, I've found it really helpful to draw symbols on the calendar. When I had to travel out of town before my girls could read, I would leave them a blocked calendar showing the various activities for each day I was gone—a bed for when they were sleeping and where, a pool for when they were swimming, a pencil for when they had school, an airplane for when I was flying back, two friends holding hands for when they had a play date. They could cross off each day, understand what was happening, and count down until my return.

The same idea works great for counting down to an exciting vacation or event in their lives.

As kids begin to read and tell time, giving them their own calendars and watches helps them track time for themselves. They can understand more about why we wait and what different units of time really mean as they wait for the next exciting moment in their family life.

Practice Waiting

Rather than wait until life demands patience from your children, we can proactively give them fun opportunities to practice waiting with happy hearts. Here are a few ideas that have helped our family grow our capacity for patience:

- **Phone-Timer Game.** Set the timer on your phone, and see how long each child can go without making a peep. Applaud them for self-control and waiting. They can do it!

- **Race to Patience.** In a yard or field, line the kids up at a starting point and make them wait for the go signal. It is so hard for them not to jump the gun. Give the prize to the one most patient at the line, not the winner of the race.

- **Cookie Test.** Put out a fresh bowl or jar of cookies, and tell the kids, "Whoever asks me about them will get one or none. If you do a great job waiting patiently, you might get two cookies after dinner." Be sure to follow through.

- **Plant for Patience.** Have each child pick out a pack of seeds and then plant them in a cup filled with dirt. Explain that it takes work and discipline to water and wait patiently for the fruits of their labor.

- **Wait a Day.** Most of the time, when our children urgently want something, they forget about it or change their minds the next day. Try having them write down their "need" or wish list. Wait a day or a week, and then see if what they listed is still important to them.

- **Pack Your Patience.** Ron's mom has the best sayings. Her gentle reminder to "Pack your patience" is one that rings in my head when we are headed for a long car ride or particularly challenging day. You could even call your entertainment bag the Pack Your Patience Bag.

Praise Waiting

Just like adults, our kids relate best to specifics. Patience looks different for different circumstances, which makes it hard to define. Sometimes patience means waiting our turn to speak; other times it means speaking calmly while we wait in line. To help children begin to recognize various ways to exercise patience, we can make a point of "catching them" when they get it right. I love to make a big deal when mine wait their turn to talk and do not interrupt. It takes a lot of self-control on their part, and I want to recognize that hard work.

Sometimes patience involves showing kindness to another person, maybe a little sister or grandparent, who isn't moving at our speed. Resisting the urge to rush others demonstrates respect and love—and it takes a lot of practice. It's difficult for kids to grasp that the world doesn't just jump and move on their demand. Mine typically race at top speed. This

Catch Phrases for **Patience**

- You can enjoy something good now or wait to receive God's best later.
- Patience is waiting with a happy heart.
- Patience means you're grateful for what you have.
- You get what you get, and you don't throw a fit.
- Some things are worth waiting for.
- When we are patient with others, they feel loved and respected.

means that when it's time to pull on swimsuits for a trip to the pool, their younger, smaller cousins aren't ready as soon as they'd like. This is a perfect opportunity to remind my girls that they aren't actually the center of the universe and they can practice waiting without making others feel rushed by their demand, "Let's go NOW!" Instead we can pass the time by packing everyone a snack or cleaning up the morning mess or playing a game. When I see them do that kind of waiting well, I jump on the opportunity to praise their patience.

Patience Is a Long-Term Project

Many of the virtues we're focusing on can lead to more obedient kids who are a pleasure to be around—and who make us look like great parents. But patience is particularly connected to how they will live out their faith.

Joke Telling.
Grab a pretend microphone and host an open-mike joke night.

This virtue affects their future ability to believe and trust in God.

I am not interested in training good little girls. I am parenting future women—adults who I pray will fully trust their Lord. Right now, they need to wait for a treat or the trip to the park. Soon enough, they'll need to wait for the right boy (not just the first one who asks them out), wait for a driver's license, and even wait for God to answer a prayer about a friendship. Just after that, they might have to wait for a husband, kids, or a dream job. I want to know they will have self-control and the ability to trust. I pray they will refrain from the common whining, "When is it my turn to get a husband?" My goal is to raise women who will not panic and overreact in their season of waiting.

By guiding our children now, we can give them a history to look back on as adults, a record of waiting and trusting God with happy hearts and seeing that patience yields the best results.

God's plan is always better than our schemes. Giving our children opportunities now to wait in the little moments prepares them to apply this critical virtue in the big moments of life.

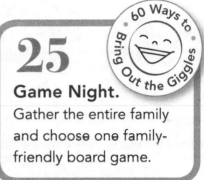

25

Game Night.
Gather the entire family and choose one family-friendly board game.

Each of us will go through seasons when we hear clearly from God and seasons when it seems He is silent. You may be in the very center of your waiting season right now. If so, I encourage you to grab hold of the words of the psalmist: "I waited patiently for the LORD; he turned to me and heard my cry" (Psalm 40:1). Do not give up. He hasn't forgotten you. And your example of patience is touching the hearts of your children.

Let's involve our kids in praying through some of our biggest moments as well as our daily decisions. We can demonstrate the power of putting our trust in God in the season of waiting for a job, a house, a diagnosis, or a next step. Our patience—living in peace, calm, and joy no matter our circumstances—reveals where our trust lies.

If we love Jesus and believe He orders our steps, our children will see this and be inspired to follow suit.

Teaching *Patience*

But if we hope for what we do not yet have, we wait for it patiently.
Romans 8:25

Virtue Definition for Memorization

Patience: waiting with a happy heart

Read in *The Jesus Storybook Bible*

"Son of laughter," page 56. God's special promise to Abraham, based on Genesis 12–21.

Questions for Discussion

- When someone is patient with you, how does it make you feel?
- When someone is impatient with you, how does it make you feel?
- What are some reasons we should be patient?

- Why is it important to wait with a happy heart instead of a grumpy heart?
- Name a time you had to wait for something and it was really hard.
- Name a time you waited and it was worth the wait!
- Ask your mom, dad, or grandparent to tell you about a time when they had to trust God and be patient with something for your family. What happened?
- Does your patience or impatience affect only your actions, or does it also affect others?
- What is coming up that we are excited about? (For example, school getting out.) How could we model patience for our friends while we wait?
- What do you do when you are frustrated and tired of waiting?

Pray

Lord, it is so hard to wait. Our family trusts You with our lives, and we trust the plan You have set for each of us. Help us remember You are in charge and You have a purpose for our lives and each step we take. Give us an overflowing amount of patience so that others might see You. Help us show patience through self-control. Help us show patience through how we love others. We love You and we want to honor You. And we thank You for the amazing blessings we receive when we trust You. Amen.

Activity: Taste the Sweet Rewards of Patience

This activity provides the perfect opportunity to practice patience. You can experiment with it several times throughout the month to give your children an opportunity to strengthen their waiting skills.

Supplies

☐ two brown bags, one small (lunch size) and one large (grocery-sack size)

☐ a few pieces of your kids' favorite candy

☐ ingredients for their favorite dessert

How This Works

Label the two brown bags with the numbers 1 (small bag) and 2 (large bag). Without any children looking on, put all the ingredients for their favorite dessert in bag 2 and close it up. Then, with your children watching, place the pieces of candy in bag 1. Do *not* let them look inside bag 2.

Offer your children a choice: "You can have something from bag 1 today. Or you can wait and have what is in bag 2 tomorrow. I promise you it is bigger and better, but you can't look inside. You'll have to trust me. What are you going to choose? Each of you can make your own choice. If you choose the candy, you may not have what is in the other bag tomorrow."

You can adapt this same concept with nonfood items. Bag 1 might have a glow-stick toy, while bag 2 contains a coupon to stay up late and go on a nighttime adventure with mom and dad to see the stars somewhere special.

After you reveal and enjoy the contents of bag 2, process some of the discussion questions as a family.

Optional Activities

PLAN a fun night out at the end of the month for the family. Talk frequently throughout the month about your expectations for "waiting with a happy heart" for the special night, and let your children know that the activities you plan will be bigger and better if they don't ask often or act impatient.

READ & DISCUSS Psalm 27:14; 37:7–9; Proverbs 16:32; Romans 12:12; 1 Corinthians 13:4–8; Ephesians 4:2.

ENCOURAGE Draw a picture of what patience looks like, and give it to the most patient person in your home or to your most patient friend or teacher.

6

Perseverance

Pressing On Through Life's Challenges

Memory Verse for the Month

I can do all things through Christ who strengthens me. *Philippians 4:13, NKJV*

What if you had the opportunity to move to London for two years? Would you say yes immediately? I think I would!

My dear friend Amber moved to London with her husband and their two boys for the adventure of a lifetime. She has the soul of a traveler, so it was no surprise to me that they took full advantage of their location to see even more of the world. I eagerly anticipated each new blog post and Facebook update. They posted a photo of their family on the coast of Spain. Then in a quaint town in France. Then off to Germany. What a thrill! I practically drooled over my keyboard as I observed their seemingly perfect, postcard-picture life via my computer screen.

But all those picturesque posts glossed over the behind-the-scenes reality of international travel. Hauling kids while navigating trains, cabs, tiny hotels, feeding issues, doctor and ER visits, food challenges, and more. The Blossom family easily could have thrown their hands up and decided to stay cozy in their London flat. But they knew they had a small window of time in that part of the world, and they didn't want to waste it. So they persevered.

26 Family Talent Show. Pick a favorite talent and perform.

Amber knows she isn't just raising two little boys; she is growing men who will know how to work hard and never give up. Amber believes that her boys will grow in their character as they learn to rely on God's strength in the hard times. I'm certain she made a conscious choice to carry on during those two years, not just for the breathtaking views and souvenirs, but because two future men were observing how their mom and dad responded when life wasn't easy.

You and I may never get to embark on such a daunting adventure, but we recognize that perseverance is so important to every child's success. Don't we want our kids to know they can do anything with Christ? That He is always there, always giving them strength? When school is hard, illness strikes, a friendship sours, or they can't run as fast as their friends, we don't want to see them derailed and discouraged. While we cannot anticipate every trial our children will face, we can prepare their hearts to persevere, no matter what.

Teaching perseverance includes instilling the lessons of working hard and never giving up. However, for Christ followers, perseverance also involves relinquishing control and realizing the ultimate strength of our heavenly Father. Our own brute strength, knowledge, hard work, and persistence can only take us so far. As an adult, I continue to bump against this tension. I believe God is honored when we work hard and put our skills to good use. However, we gain so much joy and restful assurance when we remember where our strength comes from. Whatever we face, God's got it covered. We can trust that He has a plan and He has the outcome and our entire future under control.

And that's why we can declare with Paul, "I can do all things through Christ who strengthens me" (Philippians 4:13, NKJV).

The Hard Work of Letting Our Kids Work Hard

As much as we want our kids to develop perseverance, it doesn't come easily to them or to us. In our home my chronic impatience sometimes robs my kids of a critical lesson in perseverance. In my desire to keep things moving, I am often too quick to lend a helping hand, or even do something myself, rather than let the girls figure it out themselves.

It is in my nature to take away their problems and take the easy route. Kay Wyma, my dear friend and author of *Cleaning House,* reminds me of the disservice I am doing when I take away these opportunities for my kids to grow. She wrote,

> We strive to make our children's lives easier or to make success
> a sure thing by doing it all for them. We shower them with
> accolades, proclaiming how wonderful they are—yet we rarely
> give them the opportunity to confirm the substance of that praise.
> All our efforts send the clear, though unspoken and unintended,

message "I'll do it for you because you can't" or "No sense in your trying because I can do it better and faster."

Those messages are really the *opposite* of what I want my kids to hear from me. I want them to hear the truth—that with hard work, perseverance, and discipline, they *can* do anything they put their minds and muscles to.[7]

With her powerful words in mind, I am gradually learning what not to do, and my girls are learning what they can do. Our classroom has been the pool, monkey bars, rainbow looms, boat rides, and sometimes the dinner table as we explore new foods. My heart swells every time I watch them conquer fear through perseverance.

Here's our definition of this virtue:

Perseverance: working hard and never giving up

From homework to piano lessons to baseball to ballet to reading, some sort of challenge awaits our children every day. They have a choice of whether to give up or persevere. We can help them learn the joy and fulfillment that comes with pressing on.

Of course, some of the more spirited ones are already masters of perseverance. Or maybe they are just persistent and determined, often testing mom and dad's patience and perseverance! Either way, let's embrace that quality and praise them when they use their strength of spirit for good.

Lessons in the Journey

In our home, the topic of perseverance often comes up when it is time to clean the playroom, time to go to dance class, time to do homework, or time to do essentially anything else that doesn't sound like fun at the moment. Here's a verse we have memorized as a family and refer to often: "Whatever you do, work at it with all your heart, as working for the Lord, not for human masters" (Colossians 3:23). Putting the focus back on working for the Lord helps all of us adjust our perspective.

Working hard is such an essential ingredient for character growth. Consider the impact on a generation if we succeed in raising children with perseverance ingrained in their hearts. As adults, how will they respond when a project at work is beyond their abilities? When the church needs a leader to step up? When they see a need in their community and an opportunity to help others? When a ministry needs a hardworking leader to carry a project through to completion? I pray our kids will be first in line, ready to

60 Ways to Bring Out the Giggles

27

Tug of War. Tie together scarves or handkerchiefs and start pulling.

give their all because they have a proven history of perseverance. They fully know and believe in the power of God's strength working through them. They know the rewards of working hard and never giving up. They know the rewards won't always be immediate and clear, but they can trust God with the results. They know from experience that perseverance is more about the process of growth than about the short-term outcome.

This is certainly true in our parenting. In writing this chapter, I reached out to some Lil Light O' Mine moms, women in my blog community who often discuss these topics online. I found it interesting how their comments show this virtue bubbling up in our own character growth as moms. We learn so much about our own ability to persevere as we teach our kids the value of hanging in there when things are difficult.

Here are just a few of their incredible insights.

Megan, mom of four in Denver, Colorado

In my life, motherhood is what places me squarely on the anvil of perseverance. I believe perseverance in parenting is less about the *Survivor* adage—"outwit, outplay, outlast"—and more about Christ's commissioning to "outlove" the least of these. The practice of perseverance invites me to patiently wait for God's inspired and timed response instead of relying on my immediate (often heated) emotional reaction.

Sheli, mom of Ella, a survivor of stage 3 adrenal carcinoma

On all Ella's bracelets are the words "Strong & Courageous" (Deuteronomy 31:6). Ella has taught me so much about perseverance. I remember her small body yet mature soul sitting in her hospital bed with me and telling me that everything was going to be okay. My first thought was *It's not okay, my baby has cancer,* but I would smile back at her and hug her tightly and agree that God was in control so it was going to be okay. And swallow the lump in my throat! She taught me that no matter what happens, just breathe and believe. It sounds crazy, but there were so many times in the hospital I found myself holding my breath! I also learned perseverance was like reaching inside and grasping God's peace and holding on to whatever hope existed.

Amber, mom of three in Houston, Texas

My son loves Legos, and he's pretty great at putting big sets together. He'll spend hours constructing the red Ninjago dragon,

tiny piece by tiny piece. But he wasn't always so proficient. He
would get frustrated if he couldn't find a piece or missed a step.
So we started sitting together when he'd start a new set. And I
then had a front-row seat to watch his perseverance. He'd work
and work, and then he'd get stuck at step 8 and have to go back
to step 3. He would whine a bit, as we do, ask for some help, and
then he'd just get on with it and keep working. I love this lesson.
I often think to persevere I must trudge on solo with a spring in
my step and a smile on my face, but my son shows me it's okay to
grunt out a little frustration, ask for some help, and then keep the
feet moving.

Melissa, mom of Cannon, a three-year-old fighting stage 4 cancer

When my son was twenty months old, he was diagnosed with
stage 4 cancer. We were told he had a fifty-fifty chance of survival
since neuroblastoma is one of the most aggressive forms of cancer.
Since that date we have fought with every ounce of our being,
and by "we" I mean mostly Cannon, our son! But I am thankful
beyond words for the fight, because some parents get a call that
their child has passed and they don't get to fight. I do! We do!
Perseverance to me is the willingness to fight but doing it with
grace. Believe it or not, some parents would do anything to have
one more day with their child, even just sitting beside them in a
hospital bed.

Ashley, mom of Marshall, a seven-year-old with reading struggles

We were concerned about Marshall's reading struggles from the
first time he brought his words home to practice at four years old.

Through two years of weekly or twice-weekly tutoring we were realizing that the reading was just not coming along to stay with his peers. But we read. Out loud every day for thirty minutes. Every day through the summer. Often we would have to stop a session and pray for perseverance. And patience. Marshall has grown to accept the challenge and view it for what it is. His challenges with reading don't define him and don't affect who he is; it's just a part of the uniqueness that is Marshall. He understands that hard work pays off. He also isn't so afraid of a challenge. Additionally, he realizes that just because it isn't easy doesn't mean you need to quit. Now he reads on his own to his two sisters without prompting.

The insightful comments of these women remind me of one of my favorite verses: "Not only so, but we also glory in our sufferings, because we know that suffering produces perseverance; perseverance, character; and character, hope" (Romans 5:3–4).

One of the hard parts of perseverance is accepting it as a journey. Which of us wouldn't prefer an immediate victory? But growth of character comes when we feel like giving up but choose to carry on. When we want something badly and we work hard to get it, those are the times when our character is strengthened. This is just as true for us as for our kids.

The Rewards of Perseverance

As with many of our virtues, we parents often hold the keys to the rewards of perseverance—and the repercussions of quitting. We can let our children quit or push them to keep going. It is difficult to watch them push through frustration and suffering and pain, but as Romans 5 beautifully reminds us, perseverance results in character, then hope.

I don't particularly like to see my children uncomfortable or suffering. However, when I say "No, you cannot quit; take a break, but you must finish," I am giving my children the gift of character growth and a lifetime of hope.

Sometimes we won't have a choice. They actually do have to go to school when there is a bully or a challenging class. Sometimes we do have a choice. We can snatch them right out of that swimming lesson or let them quit the basketball team. But before we go there, let's ask ourselves some tough questions: By letting them stop, are we saving them from trials that are too heavy for them to handle? Or should we push through some of the uncomfortable moments to help them build discipline? If we don't let them quit, will we eventually see their faces beaming with the pride and smiles and confidence of achievement?

28

60 Ways to Bring Out the Giggles

Handkerchief Keep Away. Toss a handkerchief around the house.

We all want our kids to be happy, but if we let their happiness and comfort drive our decisions, we rob them of a critical phase of discovery. Our kids absolutely need to explore the internal skills of perseverance, commitment, and a willingness to work hard, just as they need to explore different sports, activities, and interests. We don't want to raise adults who will one day quit a job because they didn't really enjoy an assignment or walk out of a relationship because it required some hard work.

If I can summon the internal strength and patience to let my kids ride it out, they will learn to ride it out. They will learn early that pushing through the pain brings the joy of accomplishment, even when things don't turn out perfectly. In terms of their character growth, the reward is a hopeful, confident perspective that will carry them far in life. They will learn they are more capable than they realize. Yes, they might have to work, really work. Few of us can excel with ease at everything. That is a conversation that just takes us right back to our maker, who made every one of us unique. I'm so glad He made each of us and our children so different. What a boring world it would be if we were all the same.

Sack Race. Grab an old pillowcase and race out in the grass.

I am not suggesting we force our kids to take ten years of piano lessons while they hate every minute of it. But developing the virtue of perseverance might mean finishing out a season or a year once they've committed to it. Or reading every night even when it's hard or not a child's favorite thing. I'm not promoting torture, but I am suggesting we encourage and coach, even through tears in some instances.

Past Success Brings Hope to the Present

When a child of mine confronts a new or hard task, I no longer wrestle to find the right words of encouragement. In fact I grin because we've done this about a hundred times before and I have the script memorized. I'm thankful for God's faithfulness and my child's past perseverance because I am ready for this repeated conversation:

CHILD: I'm terrible at this. I can't do it. I'll never be able to get this.

MOM: You are not terrible at this; you are new to this. Were you excellent the first time you jumped off the dock? What about the first time on the monkey bars? the scooter? What about gymnastics? ballet?

(By this time she is smiling.)

MOM: That's right. All those things you learned, and it took time. You practiced and you got really good at them. But it does take time. What is perseverance?

CHILD: Working hard and never giving up.

MOM: That's right, babe. You've got this! I'm right here.

I think all of us—moms, dads, and kids included—can actually rejoice and find glory in our past suffering because it brought us to this very point. Looking back on what we've endured gives us hope when we come face to face with a new challenge. We remember God's faithfulness and how He will help us.

Yes, it's quicker and easier to let kids off the hook or, worse, do the job for them. That is a quick fix but a terrible remedy. It robs them of the opportunity to build their character and learn to trust God to carry them through. When they hit the next roadblock in life, they will reach back for an example of perseverance and have nothing.

But if we equip them to press on through difficult tasks and seasons, they will later be able to say, "I did it. On my own. And I didn't die. I actually loved it. I remember the feeling. And I can do it again!"

Stories of Perseverance

Our own experiences of perseverance also help motivate our children to endure challenges. Believe it or not, your kids really do want to be just like you. Nearly every night my girls say, "Tell me a story, Mom! Tell me about you when you were little! Tell me a story about when we were little." I believe our trials are a perfect training ground for our children. What if our struggles became their strengths?

Maybe right now you are gripped with sadness. You feel that life isn't fair, and it just never goes well for you. I get that, I really do.

Recently I was at Starbucks sitting next to Melissa, Cannon's mom. Even as she told me about the pain of watching her son fight for his life, I could not fully imagine her journey—and can't now, but I stand in awe of her courage. Not long ago I was also with my precious friend Bobbie, a beautiful mentor and grandmother fighting stage 4 ovarian cancer. Both of these women are choosing to model perseverance for all those watching. Through their stories—how they live and hope and move forward when life isn't all rainbows and puppies—they are creating a heritage of faith for their families, who are most definitely watching. When these women draw their strength from the Lord, He receives glory.

Catch Phrases for **Perseverance**

- Our strength comes from the Lord.
- You can do all things through Christ!
- When you work hard, you please God.
- Never giving up is showing perseverance.
- I believe in you; you are stronger than you know!
- I can't wait for you to feel the rewards of this hard work.

If you are in the midst of a fierce life battle, I pray your perseverance will show Jesus to your children. When they see you doing the impossible through God's strength, the truth will nestle deep in their hearts.

If your child is the one facing life's toughest battle, remember that perseverance is transferrable. With God's strength, you can work hard and never give up. And your perseverance will point that child toward hope.

And if neither of you is facing a challenge right now, this is a perfect time to help your kids build a personal story of perseverance. The activity suggested at the end of this chapter may appear to

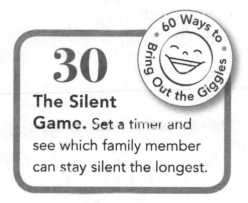

30

60 Ways to Bring Out the Giggles

The Silent Game. Set a timer and see which family member can stay silent the longest.

be a glorified field day, but it's actually a safe testing ground for practicing persistence and endurance. The idea is to help our kids learn to stick with a task when the stakes aren't too high. We put them into situations where they will face obstacles and be challenged to work hard. Their team may be outnumbered and they may be humbled, but the outcome won't determine their end-of-the-year grade or future career. This experience will provide a specific, tangible example for you and your kids to look back on and remember that you made it through with God's strength.

Let's practice perseverance alongside our children, reminding them they can do hard things through Christ. They can work hard and never give up.

Teaching Perseverance

Memory Verse for the Month

I can do all things through Christ who strengthens me. *Philippians 4:13, NKJV*

Virtue Definition for Memorization

Perseverance: working hard and never giving up

Read in *The Jesus Storybook Bible*

"The young hero and the horrible giant," page 122. The story of David and Goliath, based on 1 Samuel 17.

Questions for Discussion

- Can you be both scared and courageous at the same time?
- Name a time you worked hard to learn something new.
- Tell me about a time you jumped past a fear.
- Tell me about a time you didn't give up and your perseverance paid off.
- What is something you wish you could learn to do?

- What holds you back from doing big things?
- Do you believe you can do big things with God's strength? Like what?

Pray

Dear Lord, Your strength is all we need. We want to be strong for what You have called us to do, not to make us great. We pray that You will remind us to believe in You and believe in ourselves. When we are weak, You are strong. Lord, we want to work hard and never give up. Our family wants to be known for perseverance. For being the last one on the field, not the first to give up. We want to honor You in all our actions, behind the scenes and in front of others. Help us this month to learn through the hard moments of hard work. We love You. Amen.

Activity: Family Olympics

This is pure comedy and pure fun. You are going to have to trust me even if you aren't comfortable with getting a bit silly. The most skeptical men and women in my life have tried this activity and loved it.

You'll be gathering families to compete in a friendly, spirited little competition called Family Olympics. It's family bonding at a whole new level. Gather your team spirit and a tiny bit of competitive spirit. And definitely gather your perseverance.

Supplies

- [ ] enough T-shirts, bandannas, or other items of a specific color or theme to identify each member of your family team
- [ ] a large green space, such as a big yard or local park
- [ ] depending on which events you choose (see below for details), additional supplies

How This Works

Pick your teams. I would suggest inviting three to five families among your closest relationships, whether friends or extended-family members. This is a great activity for a family reunion. Having more than five teams competing might be hard to manage with little ones involved.

Set a date. Go ahead and mark a date on the calendar. It's ideal to schedule this for a time of day when participants won't get overheated.

Pick a place. Any park or recreational area is great, especially one with access to a basketball goal, volleyball net, or picnic tables! Or plan this as part of a weekend camping trip or mini lake vacation.

Challenge each family to come prepared with team name, team flag, and team shirts or color.

Select a Chairman of the Family Olympic Committee. "Chairing" the event involves picking the events and bringing the supplies. Since we've made this an annual event, we rotate this responsibility to a different family each year.

Select a trophy and other awards. Our main prize is a silly flamingo. You can use construction paper to make awards for specific events and for overall team spirit or other competitions. Or you might make medals out of aluminum pie plates hung from ribbons. The options are endless.

Select events. I suggest that when you're selecting from the list to follow, you include one each for moms and dads, three for the kids, and three family events. But feel free to pick whatever combination might work best, given the ages of your kids and time allotted. Come prepared to make game-day adjustments as things shift on the scene. ("Pack your patience!") And let the kids help make choices too.

Possible Mom Events

- **Mom Call.** All moms are blindfolded and positioned at a starting point. All kids start calling out "Mom!" First mom to find her kids wins.
- **Hula-Hoop.** All moms start Hula-Hooping, and the winner has the last one spinning. (My girlfriends and I absolutely trained for this ahead of time!)
- **Party Streaming.** Each mom is given a roll of streamer paper. At the start signal, participants quickly whirl their arms in a circular motion until the entire streamer is unraveled. First one with an unraveled streamer wins.

Possible Dad Events

- **H.O.R.S.E.** If a basketball court or soccer field is available, this is one the guys love.
- **Carry the Kids.** Each dad grabs a kid or two, then sprints to a cone and back.

- **Multitask Master.** Each dad is given the same series of tasks to complete. For example, change a diaper on a doll, text a grocery list shouted by mom, and install a car seat. First one finished wins.

Possible Kid Events

- **Baby Sprint.** The littlest ones crawl, waddle, or sprint from mom to dad.
- **Water on the Go.** Place water-filled buckets at one end of the field and empty buckets at the other end. Competitors use cups to transfer all the water from one bucket to the other. First team with an empty bucket wins.
- **Bucket Ball Toss.** Bring buckets and containers of various sizes, then scatter them around the field and identify them with different point values based on the distance from a throw line. Kids line up at the throw line and take aim to see who can make the most points.
- **Find That Tube.** Put round inflatable pool tubes in the grass. Participants hold small inflatable balls (or tennis balls) between their knees and hop over to drop them into their team's tube. The team that places the most balls in its tube within sixty seconds wins.

Possible Family Events

- **Line 'Em Up.** Each family has to make it across the field by lying down head to toe. One person lies down and lifts his arms above his head, then the next person lies down with his feet by the first person's hands, and so on. Keep leap-frogging until your family gets across the field. First family to the end wins.

- **Three-Legged Race.** Partner up parents and children. Loosely tie mom or dad's ankle to the child's with a bandanna. Fastest team to the finish line wins.
- **Cheese-Puff Ball Toss.** Dad suits up in a shower cap, and kids coat the entire cap with shaving cream. When the buzzer sounds, each family starts throwing cheese-puff balls from the designated line onto their dad's cap. Whichever family has the most cheese-puff balls stuck to dad's cap at the end of the thirty seconds wins!

You'll find more event ideas listed at courtneydefeo.com.

Optional Activities

PLAN Let each child pick one big thing to learn—such as how to ride a bike, tie her shoes, knit a scarf, or bake a cake. Maybe something that has felt too intimidating before. As a family, pray for strength and the courage to work hard and never give up! Then help each child tackle it. Alternatively, you might identify a family activity, such as rock climbing, that would be new and challenging for all to achieve.

READ & DISCUSS Psalm 27:14; Luke 19:1–10; 2 Corinthians 12:9–10; Galatians 6:9; Colossians 3:23; 2 Timothy 4:7; Hebrews 10:36.

ENCOURAGE Create perseverance awards or ribbons, and keep your eyes peeled for how each child displays this trait throughout the month. Hang the award on the child's door to encourage the virtue.

7

Respect

Words and Actions
That Honor Others

Memory Verse for the Month

Be devoted to one another in love. Honor one another above yourselves. *Romans 12:10*

I have a thing about kids looking an adult in the eye-balls. When I make direct eye contact with small children, it's like a secret love language of respect.

I know two little girls whom I consider role models of respect. They happen to look like American Girl dolls. (That's not important; I just want you to get a visual.) Amelia and Mallory are just a few years older than my girls. Can you picture them with their big hair bows, big eyes, big smiles, and big-time respect? From the time they were very small, these two looked me in the eyeballs and paid attention when they spoke to me. I remember noting their respectful behavior as something to aim for with my own kids when they came along.

31

Kids as Parents. Let kids respectfully impersonate their parents.

Amelia and Mallory's parents have a faith deeply rooted in Jesus Christ. I know their goal is not to have the best-behaved kids on the block but to prepare their girls for lifelong success. They know they are raising little girls to become women who one day will be college roommates and spouses and employees—and who will need to know how to respond to and interact with others respectfully.

I have the same goal in mind as I work with our girls to help them learn early in life the art of speaking to adults. I strive to model for and teach them the importance of respecting and honoring others and the things God has created, even if it means circling back to a teacher to mend an issue or to a dinner host to offer a proper "Thank you for having us." From shaking hands properly to holding the door open for others or replacing a toy that we lost, seeds of respect are going to pay off one day.

Teaching respectful behavior was a priority for my parents, and I am so grateful they took time to train me to show respect for others and for the things God created. They helped me become aware of the world around me. Through wonderful role models, positive affirmation, and some hard lessons, I learned the value of honoring others above myself. The respect I developed in the training ground of home has served me well in business interviews, corporate meetings, moms' groups, ladies' teas, classrooms, and more. I developed an internal radar that detects when the world isn't quite right. When someone needs a helping hand. When I need to hold back and let someone else speak, or when I need to think twice about how I behave toward someone.

I have benefited greatly from my parents' teaching in this area, and I want to do the same for my girls. This is the reason this virtue landed in this book: I believe respect is an integral component of bringing faith to life in our homes and in the world around us.

Some might dismiss these respectful practices as old fashioned or "southern manners." Others might believe polite manners are reserved for sweet little girls. I believe all of us, no matter our gender or where we live, are called to value others with our best behavior. Why? Because of our memory verse for this month: "Be devoted to one another in love. Honor one another above yourselves" (Romans 12:10).

God is very clear on which people we are to respect. Some? Our kind? Our family? Those who've earned it? No, "one another" means we don't get to pick and choose; this command applies to all our relationships.

Through the natural course of life, we are most likely going to encounter friends who hold different political, marital, and religious views. Do we show respect only to those we see every day? to those who think just like us? Or, as followers of Christ, are we going to honor everyone, even those who are different from our family, by treating them with dignity and respect?

Here's our working definition of respect:

Respect: honoring people and things God created

Showing respect isn't just about how we treat people; it's also about how we care for the things God has created. We can show respect through our actions and our words. If we look around, we'll find daily, almost hourly, opportunities to practice this virtue. Bringing the cart back into the grocery store, noticing and affirming a sister's homework, and being careful with dad's special book are just a few ways we can show respect for others.

My goal is for the actions and words of our family to say "I see you and I care." Through expressions of respect—maybe a simple gesture, a loving smile, or a kind note—we say, "I notice your efforts. I see your home and your things. I see your job and your hard work. I see you and I am grateful." When we respect others in small everyday ways, God's love shines deep into their hearts in a big way. We don't do these things to make ourselves look good but because we believe God calls us to honor all He has created—and most of all, because we want to honor Him.

Defining Disrespect

My girls often get glowing reports from school regarding their kindness and respect and care for others. I am honestly so grateful when the teachers affirm that some of our teaching is sticking.

However, when Ella and Larson get comfortable around others (typically family and friends), they, like most of us, tend to get *really* comfortable—and the sass and attitude and maybe a tinge of selfishness break out. They sometimes cross the line from comfortable to disrespectful quicker than you can say "Oh no she didn't!" (I have no idea where they would learn such behavior. It's only every day that I'd sort of like for life to go my way, all the way.)

In your home and mine, we might find disrespect in the way mom and dad talk to each other, in the way a sibling snatches a toy or disregards another's hard work, in a display of poor sportsmanship when a game is lost, in unkind personal comments, in carelessness with a sibling's borrowed item, or in the way a child responds to being told no. In behavior outside the home disrespect often looks like complaining, rudeness to friends, disregard for another person's home or toys, ungrateful hearts, pushing to the front or stealing attention from others, a sassy attitude, running through landscaping at a restaurant, or throwing a friend's toy.

Nothing says disrespect to me like a child interrupting an adult conversation. I love my kids. I want to hear their stories and their voices, but when I am talking to their grandfather or my neighbor and they rudely interrupt around twelve times, it truly gives me red splotches on my neck from embarrassment. We have only been discussing the rudeness of interrupting for the last seven years!

32

60 Ways to Bring Out the Giggles

Parents as Kids. Have parents respectfully impersonate their kids.

Please tell me I'm not the only one with this parental pet peeve.

I was so proud when my kids first learned to say "Excuse me, Mommy," but this achievement only led to more polite interruptions, with "Excuse me, Mommy" on continual repeat until they got my attention. We are now practicing a more silent way of patiently waiting their turn by simply placing their hand on my arm to let me know they need my attention. I learned this technique from my friend Allison, who does a great job outlining how to teach "The Interrupt Rule" on her *House of Hendrix* blog. It's working pretty well for us.

I do have to give myself a reality check when my kids interrupt. Often, I get embarrassed because I am too worried about them being obedient or how others view my success as a parent. In that moment I need to remember their age, give them grace, and avoid shaming them. I may just whisper a reminder to try the interrupt rule next time. While

I may choose to enforce a consequence if it has become a chronic issue, I've learned that my girls generally respond better to positive affirmation when it comes to character training.

It's so easy to point out examples of disrespect in our home because unkind words and attitudes, lack of appreciation, or ungrateful hearts quickly grab our attention. But what if we became laser focused on highlighting those times when they get it right? I want to be quick to praise and slow to point out failures, honoring them by letting them know I see their efforts.

My hope is that rather than restricting our children with a ton of rules, we can find kid-friendly ways to explain the concept of respect. Do our children know what God says about honoring others before themselves? Have we explained why respect for others, especially authorities, is of utmost value in our home? Do they know they are of incredible value to God—and so is everyone else?

The goal is not to develop timid kids who are fearful of putting a toe over the wrong line, but to help them establish self-control and a thoughtful awareness of their surroundings. I love how God created boys to be continually moving and adventurous. I've noticed, however, that most classrooms, libraries, homes, and restaurants weren't designed with active boys in mind, so young boys need help learning how to channel their natural energy in such places. My little buddy Charlie runs through our neighborhood full force, jumping over bushes and gathering dirt as he goes, but then he stops at the front door of my house and greets me with eye contact. He doesn't jump on my furniture or demand a drink from me. He's polite and grateful, balancing his energy with respect. Similarly, my girls are learning to set boundaries on their otherwise nonstop chatter.

With all children, we can teach them about appropriate places to play, talk, run, jump, scream, and pretend. We're not trying to force them to behave like tiny adults. Let's let our boys be all boy. Our girls, all girl!

And all of them, 100 percent kid—but with a respectful sensitivity regarding other people and their things.

It All Starts with Us

Before I had children, I worked in marketing at Chick-fil-A headquarters. It was a glorious opportunity. I worked with a group of amazing people who truly desired to honor God and have a positive influence on others. Respect was practiced at every level of the business.

One day, I noticed a tiny piece of trash on the floor in the hallway. I kept walking. After about fifteen steps, something stopped me in my tracks. Fear? Conscience? I raced back and recovered that trash before some undercover cow police got wind of my near disrespect for the greatest campus on earth.

I share that story because I think it's a great illustration of our tendency to shape up if we suspect someone may be watching. As parents, we know that little eyes and ears are constantly observing us. Realizing that I am a steward of their young lives and so am accountable to God prompts me to want to do the right thing, to make choices that honor Him.

33

Ice-Cream Shoppe. Create an ice-cream shoppe and serve up sundaes.

60 Ways to Bring Out the Giggles

They saw and heard how I responded when a retail clerk was incredibly rude. And when the patrol officer pulled me over. And when I had that difficult conversation with a teacher at school. And when a political ad I didn't like came on the TV screen. How freely was respect flowing from my mouth when I spoke to my husband at the end of a long day?

Easy Ways to Practice Respect with Your Kids

- Teach them how to shake hands properly.
- Encourage them to order for themselves at restaurants, making eye contact and saying "May I please..."
- Help pick up trash on public properties.
- Hold doors for others.
- Teach them to say "Excuse me" or follow the interrupt rule when adults are talking.
- Show the proper way to thank party hosts when it's time to go.
- Remind them of ways to respect teachers.
- Practice waiting or letting someone else go first.
- Teach them to tell the clerk "Have a nice day!" as you leave the store.
- Make a family rule that we leave places better than we found them and live it out by cleaning tables, picking up trash, pulling weeds, and more.
- Every time a relative or friend serves a meal, have the kids say "Thank you for my dinner/lunch/breakfast."
- Before you leave the house, intentionally make clear your baby-sitter's position of authority. "Who is in

charge? X is in charge. We are asking you to show her respect and be kind to your sister. We will ask about these two things when we return."

- Before you visit someone's home, explain how to be respectful by caring for their toys and things and by helping clean up when it's time to go.

- Boys can learn to stay standing until their mom sits down to eat and to open doors for others.

- Girls can learn how to give and receive a compliment.

- Practice and frequently review basic mealtime and conversation manners.

- Model how to respect others for their differences, showing inclusion and love.

- Have them pick up garbage—even if it's not yours—from the cart at the grocery store, in the parking lot, in an aisle. Let's help take care of the world around us.

- If they happen to damage or lose a friend's toy, show respect by replacing that toy.

- Talk about which things in the home are of high value and special to mom and dad and so need to be treated with special care (heirlooms, breakables, and electronics, for example).

Sometimes disrespect creeps into my words despite my best intentions. It deeply saddens me when I hear a phrase or tone of disrespect fly out of a child's mouth at my husband and I know exactly where she learned it. Rather than sitting in guilt, I repent to them and God. I am so thankful His mercies are new every morning and that I can grow in this virtue right along with my kids.

Apart from how we treat others, the way we interact with our children also leaves a lasting impression. Just because they are young and not in a position of authority doesn't mean they don't deserve to be spoken to with respect.

When I was a child, my mother made me feel like a superstar, a princess, a beloved child of God. She didn't view her children as tiny idols or place us at the center of her world. However, she listened and she looked us in the eye. She valued our wishes and our dreams and our individual strengths.

I long for my own children to grow up with the same sense of being valued. Yet all too often, I discard a piece of art that my child poured her heart into. Or I say "Tell me all about it" when everything in me is focused somewhere else. My body actions and my mood can send a message that they are not worthy of my respect and attention. I pray God will continue to work in me, helping me give my girls a glimpse of His unconditional love for them. I pray He will use me to lift them up and cheer them up, to honor them as beloved children of God. As my own precious children.

As we verbally reinforce the importance of honoring others and the things that God created, let's be sure our actions and words consistently reflect this virtue. Our children should never feel less respected than my grocery-store clerk! Instead, the very heart of God should pour from our hearts right into theirs. That takes work and self-control and, often, deep breaths during those most frustrating days.

We can do it!

Respecting Differences

Many times respecting others means confronting our own discomfort with people whose behavior or appearance is different from ours. My friend Courtney Westlake has absolutely convinced me of the importance of instilling this virtue in the hearts of our children. Courtney's daughter, Brenna, was born with a life-threatening skin condition, Harlequin ichthyosis. The disease affects this sweet baby's appearance—but doesn't change how beautiful she is to her mama.

Courtney doesn't hide or deny Brenna's differences; she uses her blog to celebrate differences of children around the world. I love how she brings honor, understanding, and dignity to so many children and families.

Many of my precious friends have adopted children whose ethnic background varies from their own. Their families get approached almost every day with bold questions and thoughtless comments. Although these words come from a place of curiosity and a desire to connect, we have to train our tongues (and our kids) to resist making comments that highlight differences in a way that separates; instead we want to celebrate how each person is made in God's image and is deeply loved by Him.

34

60 Ways to Bring Out the Giggles

Stuffed-Animal Acting. Mom or dad, grab the largest stuffed animal you can find, and start acting out a scene— funny voice required!— or read your child's book while hiding behind the animal.

God cherishes every child, every family, and every face. He created each one. There isn't a single mistake. So when we lock eyes with someone who looks different from us, do we stare? Or do we offer that person honor and dignity?

What about differences in the classroom, where our kids spend so much of their time? Some students are strong in math; others excel at art. They have different interests, different clothing budgets, different physical appearances. One of mine wears glasses. She'd prefer not to. Amid all these realities, what does it look like to show respect to classmates?

I believe we need to teach our kids the basics of showing kindness and standing up for the vulnerable. Bullying is a very real issue in our classrooms today, and I think one way we can help as parents is to make differences accepted and celebrated. Respect involves far more than sweet manners. Respect could even change a child's year or save one's spirit from rejection if we prepare our kids well. To help your kids understand respectful behavior, you might role-play a scenario with your kids. Ask "What would you do if you noticed something different about a friend?" or "What happens when your friend is sad because another friend said unkind words?"

Soon after we moved to Orlando, I took Ella to meet with a kindergarten teacher for an observation. My frightened daughter stood crying in the lobby and didn't want to go down the hallway. One girl noticed her and on her own reached out, grabbed Ella's hand, and led her along the hallway. That gesture of kindness was the start of making her feel at home in her new school. It illustrates exactly what I hope we can instill in our children by teaching them respect: the courage to make small gestures that will have a significant impact on the hearts of many.

If you've ever attempted random kindness, you know it can sometimes feel awkward. In our me-first culture, others can be caught off guard by even small expressions of respect. Let's stand out by the way we honor others. Let's teach our kids that standing out to honor God is worth it.

Respect Shows Love

One late afternoon, we were driving home from Thanksgiving break in Atlanta, with the Orlando cityscape just over the horizon. The Christmas carols were already on the radio. My husband and I grinned because the excitement was already in the air: our girls, wired from the long drive, started begging to decorate as soon as we got home. Ron and I were

Catch Phrases for **Respect**

- Try that again in a respectful way, please.
- Disrespect is disregarding the feelings of others.
- Respect is honoring people and things God created.
- God places certain authorities in our lives for a reason. We don't get to choose who we respect.
- Everything we do and say shows either respect or disrespect.
- Small gestures often show great respect.
- Every human bears the image of God and is therefore valuable and worthy of our respect.
- Do unto others as you would have them do unto you.
- Let's leave each place cleaner than we found it.

dog-tired from the same long drive, but we compromised. We said yes to putting up their little Christmas trees and a few things I could reach without getting out all the bins and making Mom and Dad too cranky.

After we followed through on our promise, we gave the girls a bath and headed upstairs to tuck them into bed. Then I had an idea: we should have a quick tree-lighting ceremony. Their little faces lit up. So, in my sweaty road-trip outfit, I slumped down by Larson's dresser to reach the cord. We started a loud countdown: Ten! Nine! Eight!... At one we shouted, "Merry Christmas!" and—*wheeee!*—the tiny lights on the crooked, purple Big Lots tree shone out. And those girls were beaming. We repeated the procedure in Ella's room. The girls jumped into bed happy, and I went downstairs and slumped tired on the couch.

60 Ways to Bring Out the Giggles

35

Stage Family.
Perform a movie theme song together.

Ron looked over with the most sincere expression and said, "You're a really great mom."

It felt like a giant hug from my Savior. I needed that so badly.

Those few simple words let me know he respected the little things I do when he is gone. He honored my efforts to make our girls feel loved and make this house a home and make it special. His respect for me with those words made me feel deeply loved, by both Ron and my heavenly Father.

This is the incredible potential of respect. It's not just about making our kids look outwardly good and well behaved. By showing respect we and our children can give a friend or a sibling or even a parent a glimpse of the Savior's love.

As I drive the girls to school, I often challenge them to show love and kindness in specific ways that honor another person or God's creation. I suggest that they let a friend go first. I challenge them to thank their teacher. I challenge them to say five "yes ma'ams" to their teacher. I challenge them to play with a lonely classmate. Anytime they are looking out for someone other than themselves, they are being respectful of others—and they bring glory to God.

Throughout the day we look for ways to make people feel noticed and appreciated for their service. We learn the names of clerks we see regularly and treat them like old friends. We leave cold Gatorades for our mail carrier, Casey, to pick up as he goes by on hot days.

I really do like the golden rule, but I like to treat others even better than I would expect to be treated. And I hope they see a glimpse of Jesus through our family.

Teaching *Respect*

Be devoted to one another in love. Honor one another above yourselves. *Romans 12:10*

Virtue Definition for Memorization

Respect: honoring people and things God created

Read in *The Jesus Storybook Bible*

"The girl no one wanted," page 70. The story of Jacob, Rachel, and Leah based on Genesis 29–30.

Questions for Discussion

- How does our family do with showing each other respect in our home?
- How can we do a better job of showing each other respect?
- Has someone ever treated you disrespectfully? If so, how did that make you feel?
- Do you feel our family shows respect to all people?
- How about those we don't know? people in our community?

- What are simple ways we can show respect to our friends, teachers, and neighbors?
- When we encounter someone who behaves differently or looks completely different, how can we show that person respect?
- What are simple words or actions that show great respect?
- How can our family show respect for the things God created?

Pray

Lord, Your Word calls our family to show proper respect to everyone—all Your people. We pray that You will draw our attention to ways we can show honor and dignity to everyone in our lives, to those we love, such as our family, friends, teachers, and neighbors, and to those You have placed in our lives as authorities. Lord, we also thank You for those we don't know yet, those who serve our family, and those who are vulnerable or different from us. May we be a family that respects and honors others in such a way that Your love is felt. We thank You for Your love. We are so thankful we are Yours. Amen.

Activity: One Fancy Feast

It's time to party! Moms of boys, moms of girls. Moms of little ones, moms of teens. You are hosting a party—at your own dinner table. One Fancy Feast. Actually, your kids are hosting a party fit for kings and queens. The goal? Learning in real life how to show proper respect to those they love. There is no better place than a dining room table set for royalty to learn mealtime manners, conversation manners, putting others first, shaking hands, and so much more!

This is not stressful; this is fun. This is a family affair. Let's not wait until you're out in the real world where a goof-up leaves everyone embarrassed. Let's practice over sparkling grape juice and even have "do overs" and "try that again" right there with your own family as your guests.

Respect comes to life through experience. Etch this memory and the virtue of respect in the hearts of your charming angels.

Supplies

- [ ] food and beverages
- [ ] everything needed for table settings—the fancier the better—for all invited guests, such as china, polished silverware, cloth napkins with napkin rings, and so on
- [ ] candles and/or centerpieces
- [ ] music
- [ ] anything to make it a special evening for your family

How This Works

Determine a night for your fancy family dinner. Let your children help determine the menu and assist with other plans in age-appropriate ways.

Of course the prep is part of the fun! As you set the table together, remind your young hosts of table manners and other details that show proper respect to those in your home. Do you eat first or pray first? Do you thank the cook? Do you compliment the cook? Do you complain about the food? Gentlemen, do you sit first? Do you offer to help? How do you clear a table? What are appropriate things to discuss at dinner?

Make "We Honor You" circles that are red on one side and green on the other to help the little ones remember to let others finish talking before they take a turn. Children can turn their circles to green when they ask a question, then turn the circles to show red. Those with red circles stay silent while each guest answers and then turn their circles over to green. Come prepared with a few questions to spark meaningful dinnertime conversation. (Try the discussion questions from this book.)

After this practice session, you might host another fancy dinner and consider inviting special guests, from teachers to mail carriers to anyone who deserves a special seat at your table and a night to feel loved and noticed.

Optional Activities

PLAN Decorate a box and insert questions people can ask at mealtime.

READ & DISCUSS Matthew 15:4; Romans 12:10; 13:1–7; 2 Corinthians 10:12–16; Philippians 2:3; Hebrews 13:17.

ENCOURAGE Go around the table at dinner and take turns finishing this sentence: "I feel respected when…"

8

Responsibility

Working Hard and
Taking Ownership

Memory Verse for the Month

Whatever you do, work at it with all your heart, as working for the Lord, not for human masters.
Colossians 3:23

I suspect that most of us as parents place responsibility high on the list of virtues we want to encourage in our children. We hope to launch our kids into the world as responsible humans. But when we step into a bedroom carpeted with land mines of Lego blocks, peek into a bathroom draped in wet towels, or endure protests of injustice and cruelty on the part of young ones asked to empty the dishwasher, the goal of responsibility seems impossibly out of reach.

Before I became a parent in real life, I dreamed that by the time my sweet children left the nest, they would be able to do their laundry, cook a meal, and even notice needs of others around them. In the midst of real-life parenting, my standards for responsibility have dwindled to "stay out of jail, don't injure any humans, and graduate high school." I'm joking. Sort of.

Certainly the real-life version of parenting reveals harsh realities. I have yet to find a child who loves work. My dear friend Kristen, who's a mom of four, entrepreneur, CEO wife, and great friend, shared a story that confirms the ugly truth about kids and work.

In spite of the fact that my brother and I live very different lives, we're thick as thieves. Brian is five years younger than me, single, and lives in Manhattan, where he's an architect at a big-league firm (whereas I'm a stay-at-home mom in cozy Orlando with our four kids). Different though we are, his parenting advice is spot on—I love to call him for counsel because his perspective is so much grander than mine: I'm stuck in the weeds…he sees the big picture. (Plus, he was a rascal as a kid, so he's experienced in this trouble-making business!)

I recently phoned him because our nine-year-old son seemed to have inherited Brian's gene for leaning on a broom and watching the rest of us work, and I was mad as a hornet. I had tried every way I knew to get our son to pitch in, but no matter what, after a few pushes of that broom, there he was, leaning on it again. I explained this alarming situation to Brian, to which he replied, "Man, you oughta be PUMPED! He's NORMAL! For Pete's sake, what nine-year-old boy LIKES to work? Three cheers for your awesome kid. Next question please?"

Brian and Kristen just beautifully captured the biggest frustration with trying to teach the virtue of responsibility. It involves work. And most human beings are allergic to hard work. Yet for some reason we expect our kids to whistle while they work and skip into the kitchen joyfully to wash dishes. The truth is that learning responsibility is hard work and being the enforcer is even harder. Have you ever grabbed all their stuff from the bottom of the stairs and hauled it up to their rooms, despite knowing you just saved them from a moment of responsibility? Have you unloaded or loaded the dishwasher just to avoid the inevitable argument that would come if you required a child to do it? Although I'm convinced we do a great disservice to our children when we do all the work for them, I often settle for the path of least resistance. It's just plain hard to make them do the work. And if I do it myself, it gets done the way I want. I love to clean up my girls' closets and the playroom, making sure everything is in its proper place. However, they will never learn how to clean up after themselves or how to clean as they go if I continue to walk behind them and make that mess disappear. How unreasonable am I to get frustrated that they haven't picked up when I keep taking away their opportunity to learn the skill?

36

60 Ways to Bring Out the Giggles

Family Fun Dinner. Pick a theme for dinner—any theme, from *Frozen* to Cowboys and Indians to An Evening in France— and as a family plan the entire dinner around that theme.

We are all going to have some growing pains this month. And that is why I love being a child of God: He has grace for you and grace for me. I have just a few short years to teach my girls that cereal bowls don't magically find their way to the dishwasher, trash cans don't empty themselves, and fingerprints aren't erased from glass. Training them in the virtue of responsibility begins now and pays dividends for a lifetime. I envision their future roommates, spouses, bosses, and coworkers thanking me with a hug for instilling this quality.

Here's our definition for this virtue:

Responsibility: taking care of ourselves and what God has given us

I think it helps us have a good attitude when being responsible ties back to everything we've been given as gifts from above—our home, our toys, our clothes, our yard, our bodies, and more. If we shift our perspective to God and His good gifts, it gives the tedious tasks more meaning and more purpose. "Whatever you do, work at it with all your heart, as working for the Lord, not for human masters" (Colossians 3:23).

When we take care of what God has given us, we are being responsible. Putting responsibility into practice can happen individually or as a family. The burden seems lighter and the tasks more enjoyable when we work together as a team, maybe with music and sometimes a little headgear. (For some reason, chores seem more fun if at least one of us is sporting bunny ears or a clown hat!) And of course, lots of praise and giggles.

How to Infuse Responsibility

I have become borderline annoying in my quest for ideas on this topic. On any given girls night out, I begin grilling my friends almost as soon as we sit down for dinner: "How do you do chores? responsibilities?" I love hearing how other families work through the struggles that seem to arise in every household. Each seems to develop a unique system and approach. Some pay kids for chores while others don't.

When I asked my Facebook community, the vast majority agreed on this approach, which happens to be what we do at our house too:

> Most common daily chores are given to each child (without pay) and taught as a part of the family system. Chores that are "above and beyond" receive payment or allowance to teach them to earn their own money and take responsibility for working toward goals.

Whether or not the parents have decided to pay their kids for completing chores, all those I connected with agree that learning how to work hard is a priority for their family. So let's look at some creative ideas for encouraging responsibility.

These are suggestions I have learned from others and adapted for our family—and they really do work. The key to success is consistency by the enforcers (that's us). Also, you may want to try just one system at a time. My kids are so confused, bless them, because I have tried too many. This month, we are going back to the Ticket Fun system and not letting up. The absolute best book and resource on this entire topic of teaching responsibility is *Cleaning House* by my friend Kay Wyma. She has some terrific ideas on how to get the entire family involved and active in this process.

Ticket Fun

Our kids really responded well to this idea from my friend Amy (mom of four). They have to complete four responsibilities each morning and four each evening to earn a "morning ticket" and an "evening ticket." (You can find rolls of relatively inexpensive carnival tickets at any party store.) As they earn each ticket, they put it in their own jar or cup. Ten tickets accumulated equals one trip to the dollar store. Our morning ticket list includes "make your bed, put jammies in the drawer, brush teeth and hair, get dressed." Our evening ticket list includes "brush teeth, wash face and hands, go potty, and put jammies on." Through this we've learned that their memory and capability is not the problem; they just needed a little motivation.

Clean Up! Clean Up!

I simply cannot clean up without music. There's a reason every preschool teacher presses Play for that popular Barney song; every kid immediately knows what to do. What's your cleanup song? Or three?

One idea to make cleanup more fun is to make a race of it. Can the playroom toys be cleaned up before mom finishes dealing with clutter in the den? And timers make everyone move faster. Challenge the kids to do the chore faster today than yesterday.

I found it's also helpful to give assignments: "Larson, here's the broom. See if you can get the entire kitchen done before this song is over." "Ella, I need you today. That Tupperware cabinet needs organizing, and you're perfect for the job."

Watch them clean at school. They can do it for you; they just need some motivation—and to learn that it's expected, not optional. Remind them that God has given your family great things and many privileges, and it's important to take care of those things.

My Lil Money Jars

I wanted my children to know from an early age that our money isn't ours; it all belongs to God, and He expects us to use it well. This means we give first, save next, and then live on the rest. Although it's a foundational principle in the Bible, we learned that from our pastor, Andy Stanley.

I wanted a system where our kids could learn financial discipline while having fun, so I created My Lil Money jars as a product for my website. Although the three jars are based on the popular "Give, Save, Live" or "Give, Save, Spend" mentality, the kids have so much fun customizing their labels for their wishes. When Ella was saving for an American Girl doll, she could write that on the label of her Save jar. If she was giving to a friend's adoption fund, that family's name was her Give label. And

37

60 Ways to Bring Out the Giggles

Grin Like It Hurts. Grin as hard as you can at one child. Get as close as you can to his or her face until giggles erupt.

we finally found a solution for those fights in the aisles of Target over how much she could spend, because her Live jar had a new label: Target. Before we even head out the door for a shopping trip, she has money to grab and she knows her spending limit.

Moms absolutely loved this product in a Pinterest, "I'm going to make it myself" kind of way. Since they caught the vision so well, I've stopped selling them and have so much fun helping others adapt the idea for their needs. In fact, for this month's activity you'll be making your own set(s)!

We Pay for More!

Do you ever feel overwhelmed because your list of incomplete projects grows with each passing weekend? I have *so* been there. But I've been happily surprised by what my kids accomplish when we approach a project as a family event or when I dangle some incentive their way. Sometimes it is absolutely necessary to pitch in and clean with no reward or incentive involved. However, I see a great return on my investment when my kids are working together toward a goal and I can teach them a new skill at the same time. With a little cash, I've motivated my girls to learn how to wash our car and organize the garage. I love building their character and their sense of responsibility while opening their eyes to the value of hard work and the value of a dollar.

You can find a number of cute chore charts on Pinterest that allow kids to choose from a list of household projects worth varying dollar amounts. The sight of that money waiting to be earned motivates them to get busy. My friend Ashley has paid her son to pick up one hundred pine cones in the yard. Older kids can learn new tasks that will serve them well into adulthood, from building fences and planting herb gardens to fixing cars, spreading mulch, pressure washing, and sewing on buttons.

There's great potential and great work in the tedious process of training kids to become responsible adults.

Instill Ownership

Watching someone else do parenting well leaves me both humbled and motivated. I try not to let my self-esteem go down in the flames of comparison but instead simply appreciate the fresh ideas I can gain from watching other moms soar in their areas of strength. My friend Ashley has always encouraged her kids to be very independent. One night I was at her house and watched her first grader do his nighttime routine. He packed his entire lunch. He marched himself around the kitchen, grabbing little containers and filling them up with one fruit, one veggie, one protein, a drink. Then he put it all in fridge for the morning. *Voila!* I was bowled over at his confidence in carrying out the task. My Ella is the same age, and I pack her lunch every day. I realized she is capable; she just needs me to put her in charge of her lunch.

I have noticed my kids respond best when they feel ownership of an area of the house and even parts of their personal routine. Everyone wants to know they are good at something. Larson loves to get a bag and gather the trash from every room. She doesn't need help. She can do it perfectly and fast. We praise her like crazy. That's her role. Ella is a master with Windex on the windows and tables. She loves it. And that girl can sort a messy cabinet with determination. I like watching them create their own nighttime rituals for brushing their hair and teeth. When it comes to straightening up around the house, they are great at organizing their personal areas and materials. Even if it takes a bit longer, Larson's determination to get her socks just right makes me smile. I love to build them up and play on their strengths.

This doesn't mean they always have to be happy when they are cleaning or working hard. It just means teaching responsibility provides a great opportunity to build their strengths and confidence. When kids feel ownership of a task, their spirits soar. And it makes your life easier because you don't have to keep reminding them. Enjoy discovering the capabilities of each child and watching chores fall off your list.

38

Family Circus. Have everyone choose a role, from juggling to clowns. Act it out and perform.

60 Ways to Bring Out the Giggles

Yes, eventually that accomplishment may lose its luster. But they don't get to stop just because they're not having fun anymore. Part of responsibility includes perseverance, working hard, and never giving up. However, we can mix up the responsibilities occasionally so they aren't tied to the same task for years at a time—and so maybe the disillusioned duster can discover that sweeping the kitchen isn't the glamour job her sister made it seem.

Another way to avoid the gnashing of teeth and crying is to offer choices. When it's time to clean up the kitchen, we might say, "We all need to clean up together. Larson, you can unload the dishwasher or clear the table. Ella, you can put the food up or dry these dishes. Let's get started!"

As noted earlier, timers are also great motivators. You might set the microwave clock alarm to a certain time and tell the kids that when it goes off, they'll know it's time to get started on cleaning the bathroom. It's strange, but they're less likely to argue with the clock than with you if you say, "Go clean the bathroom now." Another great thing about timers is that we tend to move faster when time is ticking.

Music always lightens the atmosphere, and the occasional tossing of a bowl across the room or funny football move can prompt giggles that send the tears and whines packing.

The Secret to Chore-Chart Success

After a lot of searching, I have finally found the secret to chore-chart success: consistency. The problem with all the methods I've tried wasn't the system but me. My kids have my number. They know if they just wait long enough, I'll fall off the bandwagon and start making their beds again or unloading the dishwasher because I'm quicker and they whine.

If you are one of those moms who's extremely disciplined and awesome at consistency, I want to be your neighbor and learn at your feet! (In this area, at least, I may be learning more from writing this book than you are from reading it.) But if you're like me, it's time for a little pep talk. Much like dieting, the details of the system are less important than sticking with it. And for this parent, enabling comes way easier than enforcing the chore chart. But this is part of my job as a mom. I'm here to remind my girls that we have agreed to certain jobs or chores and to get moving. I have to hold them to the consequence when they shirk their responsibility. I have to choose to let them feel the bumps that come with forgetting the lunch or the homework.

This verse reminds me of the tough work of consistency: "But let your 'Yes' be 'Yes,' and your 'No,' 'No.' For whatever is more than these is from the evil one" (Matthew 5:37, NKJV). When I say it, I've got to mean it!

This doesn't mean I won't help my kids. Of course, I love to be there for them. But part of helping them means teaching them to follow through on responsibility. This requires effort from the entire family.

Catch Phrases for **Responsibility**

- When we work hard, we honor God.
- Taking care of ourselves is our responsibility.
- Taking care of what God gave us is our responsibility.
- We can be responsible for our money, our time, our things, and what we do.
- Doesn't it feel good to complete a difficult task well?
- Our family is a team that works together.
- When you do your part around this house, it helps mom and dad so much.

The Gift of Responsibility

As you may have guessed, I tend to be a bit of a controller. I have a thing about aiming for success. If you look up *helicopter mom* on Google and read the description, it sounds a lot like me. It is my desire to help my kids toward success, but if I go about it the wrong way, I have the potential to sabotage my children.

39

Sock Skate.
Everyone, slip on some socks and start sliding in the kitchen.

I have to remind myself frequently of the powerful lessons waiting for our kids in the forgotten homework, the mistakes, the falls, the spills, and the disappointment of not making the team. It will hurt, oh it will hurt. I've never been a fan of letting my kids walk into danger, but if I jump in to save them every time, if I don't let them experience their mistakes, I place them in even greater danger. I save them from ever figuring out how to take responsibility for their own lives and their own decisions.

The apostle Paul reminds us that personal responsibility matters: "For each one should carry their own load" (Galatians 6:5). It's in the process of character growth that we meet Jesus. In our times of struggle, we learn to lean into God and He refines us.

If we continually serve as our children's internal compass, their conscience, their bag packers, their dishwashers, their mess sweepers, we rob them of the messy work of refinement. But if we let our kids experience the natural consequences of their choices while they are young, the temporary hurts will heal while they are in our care, and they will gain strength for the long haul of life. We will dust them off and prepare them for the bigger bumps of their lives by training them how to think, how to turn to God for guidance.

Let's commit to helping our kids learn responsibility through a biblical lens and through the choices we make as a family. This virtue will take deeper root every time you make your son "do the right thing" and apologize to that child, when you re-

40

60 Ways to Bring Out the Giggles

Thumb Wrestle. Let the thumb wars commence!

quire your daughter to pay for that broken item or do her homework again. Your kids may pout or call you a "mean" mom or even worse. But by requiring them to take responsibility for their actions now, you are doing the good and important work of helping them grow into adults who take ownership in their friendships, in marriage, and at work. And then one day they will hug your neck as they get promoted, noticed, and honored as the employee of the month. When they develop a reputation as the neighbor people can count on, the friend full of integrity who is always called first.

I am praying for your strength today, for your courage to fight through these early years when teaching your kids responsibility seems almost impossible. I pray our sweet heavenly Father will reveal a little smile of pride from one child who did something on his own. I pray one child will pick up her dinner dishes without being asked and you will know your work matters. I pray that our desire for them to grow will outweigh our desire to be needed by them. I pray that you and your husband will cheer each other on with a bigger prize in mind, confident that whatever we do, we are working for the Lord. He is honored and glorified in everything. Every wet diaper and every Lego spill, every mistake by our kids and by us is an opportunity to live out the virtue of responsibility. You are amazing. Don't give up.

Teaching
Responsibility

Whatever you do, work at it with all your heart, as working for the Lord, not for human masters. *Colossians 3:23*

Responsibility: taking care of ourselves and what God has given us

"The warrior leader," page 108. Joshua and the battle of Jericho, based on Joshua 3 and 6.

- Can you name someone older than you who is very responsible? How can you tell?
- What should we do when a job we've been given isn't fun or it's too hard?
- Is God honored when your attitude is right?
- What does it mean to be a good steward?
- Who is honored most when we work hard?

🌀 Pray

Lord, our family wants to honor You with our work. We are responsible for everything You have given to us. We are stewards of our money, our time, and each item You place in our hands. Please help us have self-control, discipline, and determination as we work on responsibility in our home. Please give us patience with each other as we learn. We want to work for You in everything we do so that Your love shines bright for others to see. Amen.

Activity: Make Your Own My Lil Money Jars

As I mentioned, we've found that this system works great for setting families on a journey to financial responsibility. Each child can make his own set of jars, or the family can have one set to share. Allowing the kids to personalize the label for each jar gives them an increased sense of ownership—and they love watching those coins accumulate!

Supplies

☐ three jars for each set you plan to make

☐ labels (paper is fine, but vinyl or chalkboard labels offer more flexibility for changing after a child reaches a goal)

☐ markers or chalk

How This Works

The first jar represents the "give" aspect of financial responsibility—being generous with the blessings God gives us. The second is for "save," and the third is for "live" or "spend." In our home we use labels made out of vinyl or chalkboard material so kids can customize and change the labels in ways that motivate them. If our kids are giving to a certain fund or ministry, they can write that on the Give label. Or if they are saving toward a certain big toy, they might name that item on the Save jar. The same with the Spend jar; they might label it Candy or Target.

Once you have your plan, simply label the three jars, and kids can begin placing money in them according to the percentage breakdown you agree on as a family. You might begin a discussion of proportions in each jar by sharing how you tithe, that the first 10 percent or even more always goes into the giving jar. It's important to explain the order. We give first, then save, and then we can live on the rest.

Where do they get the money? Some of it might come from birthday or holiday gifts, but you may also want to create earning opportunities. Challenge your kids to take responsibility for extra areas in the home. You can decide the amount that seems appropriate to pay for each task and how often. Or if you use the ticket plan described earlier, a certain number of tickets might earn a financial reward rather than a trip to the dollar store. There are so many options. Ask friends how finances work in their homes.

Obviously, taking care of money is just one way we can bring our kids' minds and hearts into the game of stewardship. Be sure to enjoy all the optional activities this month so you can help your kids further engage with the rewards of responsibility.

Optional Activities

PLAN a night to list all the main chores and responsibilities for the home and how your family can work as a team to take care of the things God has given you. Also, list the "above and beyond" duties that kids can choose to earn extra rewards.

READ & DISCUSS Psalm 15:1, 4; Romans 12:12; 1 Corinthians 14:40; Galatians 5:24–25; 6:5.

ENCOURAGE Keep a lookout for one teenager who is extremely responsible, maybe a baby-sitter who always cleans up or a teen boy who mows lawns to raise money. Interview that person with your kids. Invite the teenager into your home, and learn about how she developed the virtue of responsibility. Give a small gift—freshly baked cookies or a small bouquet of flowers—to encourage such great behavior.

9

Service

Meeting Needs with Our Hands, Feet, and Hearts

Memory Verse for the Month

Serve wholeheartedly, as if you were serving the Lord, not people. *Ephesians 6:7*

An experience in a tiny hospital chapel with my family forever sealed my impression of service. I'll never again look at a bowl of water and dishtowel the same way.

Let me explain.

Many of the ideas in this book developed through conversations and mile-long texts with my best friend Katie. She will read a verse or a devotion and text me. I will read something and text her. And then we will jump to put our new insights into action. I love how she makes me a better mom. We try new things together and dust each other off when we stumble.

One day, Katie posed a question that changed my mind-set on service: "What if, every six to eight weeks, our church small group can-celled our socials so we could serve together?" I was immedi-ately excited by this idea of using community to regularly gather and serve—and having our kids involved was the very best part. While I had often experienced and long embraced the idea of in-dividual service as well as work-ing alongside my husband, the idea of serving as a group and—even better—as a group of fami-lies shifted my view of service. I was thrilled that we could work together while shaping the hearts of our children, exposing them to the great privilege of loving others and honor-ing God.

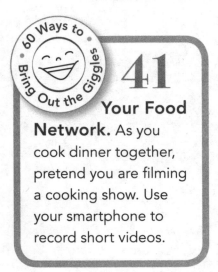

60 Ways to Bring Out the Giggles

41 Your Food Network. As you cook dinner together, pretend you are filming a cooking show. Use your smartphone to record short videos.

Like-minded adults can gather in the name of Jesus and change lives, but what happens when life-minded families gather in His name? I be-lieve generations are motivated. Communities are shaken and the very presence of the Lord shows up. Katie and I ran with her suggestion, and we each took steps to schedule our first service project.

It is actually hard to find organizations that open their doors to young kids serving, but Yvonne with Bags of Blessings is a mom of four and a woman absolutely on fire for God. She understands the power of giving to others through service.

She met us at Florida Hospital with all the supplies for our project.

She spoke to our kids about the patients they would visit on the cardiac floor and about the "bag of blessing" they would each carry to their designated patient. She explained how to pack each bag with something that appealed to each sense: a candle to smell, a CD to hear, and a blanket to touch, for example. Then we packed together and prayed together. This approach allowed the kids to use their hands, and in turn, it engaged their hearts in the process of service.

Nervous kids gain confidence through each other. Peer pressure is a good thing in this context. Although they didn't know exactly what to expect from their patient visits, they weren't alone, and they knew they were doing something important together.

As the elevator doors opened on the cardiac floor, chills came over my body. I just said, "Yes, Lord." I suspect that's the secret to heartfelt service: all we have to say is yes. We had no idea what patients waited for us or what they needed, but we had tools to make them feel just a touch better and noticed and appreciated. The special part is that people generally welcome kids. They are skeptical of adults and our motives, but they love the pure joy, love, and innocence of a child.

In each room my kids explained what was in the bag and said, "Feel better!" Then we were able to pray over patients and give them encouragement. The children were nervous and sometimes clingy, but they did it. They experienced the beautiful act of serving to honor God and His amazing people.

At the end of our time on the cardiac floor, we were asked to gather in the chapel. I had no idea what Yvonne had planned to wrap up this visit. She and her husband, the CEO of Florida Hospital Altamonte, stood beside their hospital chaplain, Pastor Sergio, and sweetly affirmed our kids and our families. They spoke about the power of service and what the hands of our children had just accomplished in Christ's name. Then, to mark the occasion and encourage the children toward a lifetime of service, they asked each child to step up to the altar. As our precious young children walked up and placed their hands over a sacred bowl used many times before, Yvonne's husband poured holy water over their sweet, cupped hands and Yvonne quietly spoke a blessing over them. I fought back tears as I captured each moment with my camera.

Chills covered my body as my friend affirmed and thanked each child. Then she did the same for each parent. She looked us in the eyes and blessed our work and our faithfulness to the Lord. When it was my turn, our eyes locked in a moment I just can't fully describe. We were two followers of Jesus bonded in service and grateful for each other's role in the journey.

All Are Called to Serve

Have you ever felt that some people are just called to a life of service? While it does seem God has uniquely gifted certain individuals to be nurses and caretakers, teachers and social workers, the truth is that all of us who follow Jesus, without exception, are called to acts of service. Our Savior came down from heaven for precisely this purpose: "For even the Son of Man did not come to be served, but to serve" (Mark 10:45). He calls us all to do the same. And we can, in more than a million ways.

Though how we serve will look different depending on our family's skill set and passions, the definition remains the same for all of us:

Service: using our hands, feet, and hearts to honor God and love others

We are God's plan to meet the needs of people. No matter what your gift, how much money you have, or your age, He wants you. All you have to do is be willing. And it won't always look like a big group event to serve the sick. Service can simply be noticing a person in need and stepping in to help. If we practice enough, we will begin to wake up with a radar switched on for others. We instinctively look to see who we can serve and help in small ways so that others see God's love. Service becomes who we are and not what we do; it's just how we operate.

There is so much to do in our own neighborhoods, churches, schools, communities, and all across the world. What excites me most about this chapter is that we get the opportunity to open our children's

42

60 Ways to Bring Out the Giggles

Wheelbarrow Race. Take this one outside. Let one child be the wheelbarrow, hands on ground, while one parent holds the legs. Race another parent-child pair!

hearts and eyes. We get to ignite in them a thirst to serve. We can teach them that God doesn't call the strongest, richest, or oldest; He calls those who are willing. And our family is willing because we love God. As we invite our families into the beautiful experience of serving, I can't wait for the changes we will see—in our children, in the people they serve, and in ourselves.

We Are Servant Leaders

One day, I made the dreaded late-afternoon stop at Publix. As soon as we went in, the girls began fighting over the seating arrangements for the racecar cart. While barking threats through my grinding teeth, I noticed an elderly lady struggling with her cart. I left my kids to fight, climb, push, and shove each other and walked over to separate her cart from the one it was stuck to. That dear lady thanked me with a huge smile. Like the well-trained former Chick-fil-A employee I am, I said, "My pleasure, ma'am."

When I turned around, the girls were silent, no longer fighting but smiling. Ella's beaming look of approval told me everything I needed to know. I saw "Great job, Mom" written in her eyes. I saw it register in her heart what a tiny gesture can do. I was so very encouraged.

Face-Painting Night. Pretend it's the circus or a fair, and create artwork on each other's face.

Sure, day to day my kids can make me almost pull my hair out. However, I know it's critical to exercise the daily discipline to teach them how Jesus would treat others. I want them to love and serve others, in the small ways and in big ways. My desire is to raise women who willingly serve even when they don't get the credit or recognition. I look forward to seeing them as adults who use their hands, feet, energy, time, and money in ways that honor God's name above their own.

To get there as adults, they need their dad and me to teach them service now. It's important for our kids to realize that serving others in the name of God is a privilege—and we can show them it's not reserved only for big people who undertake big things. As Mother Teresa so often taught, we can do "small things with great love, ordinary things with extraordinary love."[8] We can sweep a porch, carry in groceries, make a meal, and give someone a ride. If we will listen to His whispers and nudges, we will begin to experience the true joy of life: the goodness of following Christ and knowing we play a role in His plan to love the world.

How transforming it is for our children to witness—and experience for themselves—the privilege it is when God uses our acts of service to show His love to people. My friend Kylie had a recent mind-set shift from seeing her role as disciplining to discipling. Her days and her ways began to look very different when she realized we are discipling our kids to learn how God works through us. We are His plan to light up the world.

We can show our kids the nature and privilege of service through the way we use our individual gifts. My friend Katie serves through her meals. My kids know her gifts well and scarf them down with joy. My friend Joy serves couples with her passion for marriage by mentoring them before they walk that aisle. My sister serves through her words of

Catch Phrases for **Service**

- Jesus came to serve, not to be served.
- We can use our hands, feet, and hearts to serve others!
- Service is one way we show God's love to His people.
- God treasures the lost, the fatherless, the poor, the broken, the hungry.
- We each have a gift; let's use it to serve others and honor God.
- We don't need to love what we are doing to serve well.
- Let's watch today to see who we can show God's love to.
- Let's watch to see who we can help today.

affirmation and her ability to make God real to friends she meets along the daily mom journey.

The Bible, through the teaching of the apostle Peter, confirms that each of us has a gift and we can use it to serve: "Each of you should use whatever gift you have received to serve others, as faithful stewards of God's grace in its various forms" (1 Peter 4:10).

From picking up someone else's trash to putting away carts in a parking lot—there are small ways every day that we can serve all God's people and model a life of service for our children. We model service in the way we joyfully hold a door, let another car go before us in the carpool lane, or stay late to prep a classroom so that same teacher isn't late for her family. As we model, they see. As they join, they experience. As they serve, they honor their King.

We Don't Belong on the Sidelines of God's Story

While service can and should be practiced through daily, simple acts, it can also include reaching beyond our immediate circle to show God's love around the world. My friend Kylie, a dedicated wife and mom of four, is wildly passionate about serving orphans. She doesn't let barriers of age, health risks, traveling money, or anything else get in the way of what God has called their family to do. I want you to hear her compassion straight from her heart:

> My husband, John, grew up a missionary kid in Brazil from
> age two to twelve. It always excited me to think of a life like
> that, exposing our kids to how big God is outside of comfort-
> able America. We decided we aren't going to let the fact that we
> aren't "missionaries" stop us from raising our kids missionally.

Now of course this can and should be done inside your city, state, or country. But God had grafted Africa in the fabric of my heart, and with our youngest two children being from Congo, we knew this was the continent for our family. Our heart was to expose them to the brokenness and beauty, the poverty and richness of spirit, the tragedy and triumph of life there.

Taking a four-year-old to Kenya seemed a little crazy, and we heard it a time or two after booking the trip. But where some see risk, I see benefit. I hope that our kids see that in our family we choose obedience and compassion over our safety. We later took our seven-year-old daughter as well. The temptation is to shelter, to wait until they're "old enough" to understand what they'll encounter. We've decided the contrary is true for us. Barriers were shattered. Our four-year-old son was walking through the slums of Kenya kissing and high-fiving kids in tattered clothes and crusty faces. Our daughter strapped a baby to her back in true African fashion, played with children in an orphanage, helped prepare dinner with a family living with HIV, and built a fire with boys on the street. This is not because we are stellar parents but because our God is a big God who wants us to find him where he told us he would be: at the bottom of the pile with the marginalized, the broken, the least of these.

We feel like the best way to cultivate compassion and generosity in our children's hearts for the least, the vulnerable, and the orphan is to expose them to that world. I don't want my kids growing up thinking everyone lives at the level we do, that food is always in excess, and that their biggest problems are what to wear or that I made them apologize to their sibling. I want my kids to have a context for how much of the world lives. I want it to be an ongoing discussion in our home. Not just a guilty comment at dinner about hungry children but a memory, an experience, a connection they've made. I don't want my kids to just sit on the sidelines of God's story. I want their heart to follow their treasure. I want their treasure to be what God treasures. And he treasures the lost, the fatherless, the poor, the broken, the hungry.

It is so easy for me to get caught up in "stuff," making memories with fun date nights, good devotions, making sure our playroom is stocked with toys. These are good things but they are not the ultimate things. When we serve as a family, a reset button is hit in our hearts, a re-ignition of the passion God has put deep inside and a fading away of temporary and petty worries that cloud my mind.

Safety is a mirage of control. I realized I cannot clench my fingers around my children as if they were mine to hide and shelter under my wings of safety. They were designed to be arrows of the Lord, to pierce darkness, to fly wildly into danger bringing light and life that Jesus offers. I would be withholding them from God's purpose if safety is my main goal.

This is the adventure God has called us to. A wild adventure, where discomfort and joy collide, where safety goes out the window and dependence is required in a way we have never known.

Kylie and her family are a terrific example of service. Her passion for orphans and Africa has widened our perspective and influenced our family. And you know what? It's so easy to play the mom comparison game and get down on myself. *Am I doing it right? Am I good enough? Why haven't I gone to Africa? Should I be adopting?* We might one day. We might not. The truth is that we are all different but all gifted with ways we can serve the Lord.

Service can look different for each family, but each family is called to service. Let's not miss out because we were sitting on the sidelines of God's story!

Family Service Ideas

I believe in family time as often as possible. When our kids do something they enjoy, it increases the likelihood they'll want to do it again. So why not make service something we do together and make it fun? Here are a few things your family might enjoy trying over the years. And this month's activity will give you a chance to serve together right away.

Around the Community

Weed the flower beds at church, shovel snow for a neighbor, mow a neighbor's lawn, pack food or build boxes at a food bank, serve a meal together at a homeless ministry, bake cookies for someone in need, hold a door, bring a cold cup of water, clear trash. The opportunities are almost endless.

What You Have, Where You Are

God absolutely convinced me of this concept a month ago with my girls: just say yes and be willing, and He will take care of the rest.

My friend Kylie was raising funds for their new Care for AIDS center. I knew we could write a check to help, but I also knew I would miss the chance for my girls to ever realize what was happening. So I showed them the video about the center, and we had a brief brainstorm session to think of ways we could help. Our family quickly decided to have a porch sale and agreed to give 100 percent to the center.

Over the next few days, they chose what to sell—books, shoes, toys—running frequently back upstairs to grab something else they wanted to sell. I beamed with joy while watching them organize and plan to sell their own things for the good of others they may never meet.

We prayed the night before the sale for traffic and people. That morning we put signs on the ends of the street, the girls set up a lemonade stand—and God started moving. I couldn't believe how many people came. We raised over one hundred dollars in just two hours! That is a ton of money when everything was priced so low—twenty-five cents for books, a dollar for shoes. But people got excited about participating as they read the sign about the center. One lady bought a three-dollar item and left a twenty-dollar bill. The girls were giddy as they saw the effects of their service. We texted Kylie and her kids photos of the cash.

Here's the point: you can take what you have where you are and make a difference. Add some prayer and some lemonade, and you'll have a memorable day that honors God and serves others, maybe even across the world.

Connecting with Children Elsewhere

A number of organizations do a terrific job of serving the needs of children around the world. And—bonus!—connecting with them allows our children to broaden their perspective of how their hands, feet, and hearts can make a difference to those in need. Through Compassion International we sponsor two girls in Haiti whose birthdays are close to my girls' birthdays. I was prayerful and careful in choosing who to sponsor, with the idea that we will visit them one day. Through our correspondence, we aim to let these girls know they are loved and supported by our family for a lifetime. And we aim to inspire our own girls to hop on a plane and go serve their community one day. We already discuss how we serve through our letters and through our financial support, which can help them acquire a goat and water and food and clothes.

60 Ways to Bring Out the Giggles

44

Picnic Dinner. Make a regular dinner fun by eating on a blanket in the yard—or in the living room, if the weather is uncooperative.

Other great organizations you might want to consider for your family service efforts include World Relief, Children's Hope Chest, Holt International, Feed My Starving Children, and Samaritan's Purse.

Leading Small Groups

When you lead, you are accountable. As parents we know well how being responsible for our children sharpens our faith regularly; the same is true for our kids when they have an opportunity to lead others. In earlier seasons of my life, I had the privilege of leading a group of girls just a season below me. This responsibility challenged me to a higher standard, knowing others were observing my example. I would love to see my girls serve others by leading at VBS, in youth group, in small groups at church, as camp counselors.

60 Ways to Bring Out the Giggles

45

Parents Challenge. Safely prank kids by rolling their rooms or short-sheeting the bed.

Our acts of service plant seeds of God's love in the hearts of our kids and those they serve. We may never see in our lifetime the impact we have on others. Sometimes we will feel unappreciated, unseen. That's okay. "Let us not become weary in doing good, for at the proper time we will reap a harvest if we do not give up" (Galatians 6:9). We serve not to be seen or to be praised but because Christ served and because we are His plan for showing the world His love.

And sometimes we do get a glimpse of the results when God uses our lives to show others His love. What an honor.

Let's keep our eyes peeled. Who can we serve today?

Teaching *Service*

Serve wholeheartedly, as if you were serving the Lord, not people. *Ephesians 6:7*

Service: using our hands, feet, and hearts to honor God and love others

"The Servant King," page 286. The Last Supper, based on Mark 14 and John 13–14.

- What are some examples of Jesus serving others in the Bible?
- What are different ways we can serve others?
- Describe a time someone served you humbly, expecting nothing in return.

- Who serves our family well?
- Can you think of anyone who could really use an extra hand?
- What are your unique gifts? And how do you think God can use your gifts for service?

Pray

Lord, You are the King of kings. And You created this entire universe. So the way You entered this world as a baby in a manger and then served so humbly is amazing. We want to honor Your Word and serve the way You served. We want to be Your very hands and feet. We want to be the first to meet the needs of all those hurting in our communities. Lord, please use our service to honor and glorify Your name above all others. Amen.

Activity: In This Group, We Will Serve

There is power in numbers. Our kids gain confidence as they try something new when their friends join in. As I described in our experience with Bags of Blessings, doing a service project together is powerful for adults and children alike.

This month, your task is simple yet profound. Gather a group of at least three families and serve someone, anyone. You can do it formally through a ministry, or you can try one of the ideas listed below.

Supplies

☐ depends on the specifics of your project (see suggestions below)

How This Works

Designate a "Service Chair" for your group of friends or church small group. The Service Chair can research opportunities in your area, looking for organizations that are already meeting needs and that your group can support. Or the Chair can identify a specific opportunity that's just waiting for someone to step up and help. If you make this an ongoing event, you can rotate this role among the adults, with a new project every six to eight weeks.

Ideas for Group Service

- **Helping Hands.** Find a single mom or military wife whose husband is deployed, and take over for a day! Paint, do yard work, whatever she needs. Husbands can finish her honey-do list, kids can organize toys and clean, moms can organize, cook, and do laundry.
- **Brighten Your World.** Contact a local school or charitable organization to see if they have an area where they'd like some flowers planted or a wall that needs to be painted—anything to help make their world a little cheerier.
- **Feed Your Neighbors.** Contact a local homeless ministry, and find out what night your group can take over that kitchen. Help prepare the meal, and have the kids out there

serving and passing out napkins—or doing whatever is needed.

- **Serve Your Church.** Contact your church, and explain that you have X able bodies and X volunteer hours and simply ask, "How can we serve you?"

Optional Activities

PLAN one evening to sneak out to serve a neighbor. Don't tell the neighbor. Just mow a lawn, sweep a porch, or leave a fresh pot of flowers. Or a hot fresh meal.

READ & DISCUSS Mark 9:35; Acts 20:35; Galatians 5:13–14; 1 Peter 4:10.

ENCOURAGE Think of a person who serves your family humbly all year long—teacher, pastor, grandparent, coach—and find a way to encourage that individual.

10

Humility

Giving God and Others Center Stage

Memory Verse for the Month

Be humble, thinking of others as better than yourselves. Don't look out only for your own interests, but take an interest in others, too. *Philippians 2:3–4, NLT*

I am not really a big rock-star fan (except for that New Kids on the Block phase in my teen years). So I don't really do concerts or get excited about waiting for a show or seeing a certain singer. My celebrity fascination is reserved for great authors and speakers.

One of my favorites of the last decade is Bob Goff, author of *Love Does*. His book had an impact on me like few things I've ever read, so when he came to Orlando to speak, I jumped at the chance to hear him. It just so happened that my friend Kylie was to introduce him at this conference. She got me a seat right next to her. When I arrived, I expected him to be back in the greenroom like all big speakers. But there he was, right up front. Just like an ordinary human, he was walking around and saying hi and posing for photos with people. I watched him laugh warmly and hug people. He looked genuinely excited to see new people and faces. He heard their stories. He loved. Everything about Bob Goff said humility.

60 Ways to Bring Out the Giggles

46

Family Dance.
Choreograph a family dance. Record it and send it to grandparents.

As one of the major speakers of the conference and a *New York Times* best-selling author, he absolutely could have been backstage meeting a few VIP visitors and gathering himself before his talk. Instead he was meeting his fans and giving people like me a chance to say hi and thank him for the impact of his words. And when he started his speech, guess what he did? He invited people standing at the back of the crowded room to come up and sit on the floor in front or sit on the stage with him. After the talk, guess what he did? He stayed right there and spent time with whoever wanted to talk or take photos with him.

Observing Bob Goff in person impressed me as much as reading his book. I am so drawn to people like him who invest their lives in showing off the greatness of their God instead of worrying about how they look. They embody the challenge of Philippians 2:3–4: "Be humble, thinking of others as better than yourselves. Don't look out only for your own interests, but take an interest in others, too" (NLT).

Humility is a vital companion to many of the virtues in this book, including service, generosity, love, respect, and responsibility. Putting it into practice this month will give us opportunities to revisit those other aspects of life that are so important to our children's character development.

Living Out Humility 101

To be honest, my kids (and their mommy) start out most days thinking, *What about me? When will it be my turn? When do I get what I want? Who's going to notice me?* It's the rare person who does not occupy center stage in his own life, which is why our definition for this month tackles that problematic perspective head on:

Humility: giving God and others center stage

It takes practice to start thinking of others first and to consciously give God center stage. This is not something that comes naturally to our prideful human natures. But humility is important to God, so it's important to us. If we are families that follow Christ, we need to get really good at putting others before ourselves.

We can start by letting our children know this virtue is of high value in our homes. We can help them recognize how boasting and arrogance crush relationships—and we can help them experience firsthand the peace and joy that follow the wise choice to honor others. And, be quick to point out this Christlike trait since it's hard to define and a big word! It's not as easy as kindness or love to grasp for our little ones.

I love to invite my children into situations where they can practice humility. When a friend is doing really well and I see jealousy registering on the faces of my children, I might say, "Hey, girls. Aren't you so proud of Anna Wells? She is doing great! Let's run over and hug her. I love encouraging our friends!"

When Ella chose not to participate in the school talent show, we decided to make bouquets of paper flowers for all her friends who took to the stage. It shifted the focus off her and placed it on others. She was so delighted to cheer them on and deliver her flowers at the end.

Learning now that the very best friends put others first is a lesson that will serve our children well the rest of their lives.

Funniest Family Photo. Take a creative and funny group photo, and send it to family or friends with a challenge to send back their most creative effort. Props and hats encouraged.

This weekend some dear friends came into town, and we had an opportunity to practice putting others center stage. We live in a very flat neighborhood in Florida, so basically all months of the year, we scooter. My girls have honed their scooter skills to such an extent that they have now combined ballet with the scooter and call it "scoollet." Mind you, they are recklessly fearless and are sporting roughly one hundred Band-Aids per leg.

Our visitors, the Thomas family, had not had the same opportunity to practice on scooters, so within moments of their arrival, the beaming DeFeo girls realized they had a leg up on their dear friends. I didn't want to smother their joy in mastering this skill. However, I knew they'd be tempted to boast and whiz past their less speedy friends unless I helped them consider how they might feel if the situation were reversed. "How would you feel," I asked them, "if you were trying something new that your friends could do pretty well?"

My girls did fairly well with this challenge, but I had to be diligent about pulling them aside to ask them to cheer on their friends and convincing them to wait for the others instead of racing ahead. I wanted them to practice letting others have center stage for a bit. I watched like a hawk for boasting and bragging—that behavior doesn't fly on my sidewalk. At one point, a child of mine tried to time races so she could prove she was the fastest. Like an idiot, I started timing. Then I realized the scheme and quickly put the kibosh on that unhelpful game.

I am delighted to say those Thomas kids had a weekend of perseverance. They soon owned those scooters with their awesome skills. I was so

Catch Phrases for Humility

- God designed each person with unique strengths.
- More humility, less pride.
- Life is measured not by our successes and wins, but by how much we give.
- We please and glorify God by doing the right thing in our finest hour and worst hour.
- We have a chance every day to humble ourselves through generosity, service, gratitude, and kindness.
- Let's put others before ourselves.

proud of those kids for working hard and never giving up (chapter 6). And my girls had a workout in putting others' needs ahead of their own, with frequent reminders from Mom. I don't have a pretty bow to put at the end of this story. My girls didn't instantly become models of humility. But the experience reminded me that taking a backseat to others isn't natural, and as parents we have to seize those teachable moments.

Kid Comparison Trap

Of course, if we're going to help our children give center stage to others, we first have to conquer our own tendency toward one-upmanship—a particular challenge for many moms. Gather a few of us and our off-spring on any playground, and you have a breeding ground for comparison. One three-year-old dangles from the jungle gym by one arm before executing a triple-flip dismount. Another three-year-old won't budge from the top of the slide, where he's paralyzed and crying with fear. Immediately the moms are sizing each other up, making judgments about the other person's parenting choices and assumptions about her child.

Such comparisons rarely direct us toward humility and love. Instead they lead us—and our kids—to feel either superior or inferior, neither of which is healthy or productive. Psalm 139:14 is such a beautiful reminder that God made our kids unique for a purpose: "I praise you because I am fearfully and wonderfully made." In addition to correcting our perspective on our children's differences, that verse reminds us not to take credit for their God-given strengths.

Here is my prayer for me and for you when comparison threatens to undermine our choice for humility about our children:

Lord, let their WEAKNESS be the very thing that draws them to You.
Lord, let their STRENGTH be the very thing that draws others to You.

Each child's worth is not defined by her strengths and weaknesses, by what she can or cannot do; our children's value is rooted in God's unshakable love for them. He sees them as precious, and so they are.

Tips for Parents with a Heart for Humility

- Give God credit (center stage) when your efforts succeed.

- Practice saying, "I'm sorry, I was wrong."

- Share your struggles and weaknesses with your kids.

- Be on the lookout for how you can encourage your kids' friends—and their parents—by affirming their gifts and positive behavior.

- When things go well, consider how to deflect praise in front of your kids.

- Help kids accept team wins and losses with equal grace and humility.

- When your child scores, clap and cheer proudly.

- When another member of your child's team scores, clap and cheer just as proudly.

- Spend time with humble leaders or read about some.

- Point out to your children those individuals who stand tall with confidence yet lead humbly.

- Commit to do your best and trust God with the rest.

When our children get too puffed up by a strength, let's be quick to remind them that it is a gift from God and He alone deserves all the glory. If they get down on themselves for a weakness, let's help them see it as perfect grounds for depending on Him, a way God can display His strength in their lives.

From scooters to math to reading to soccer, our kids will soar at some skills and flop at others. Let's train them to have a biblical response to both: a humble heart grounded in God's love for them.

Keep your eyes peeled. Opportunities are scooting by daily!

Humility Is Not for Wimps

Out of fear of encouraging pride, some parents may choose to withhold praise from their kids, but I really think that's a misunderstanding of humility. Raising our children to be humble doesn't mean beating down their self-esteem or breaking their egos. Humility is not about having a pitiful level of self-worth.

Yes, in praising our kids we risk raising individuals so confident in their own abilities that they don't need God, or anyone else for that matter. (*American Idol* suggests that a few thousand parents forgot to be honest with their kids about their strengths and weaknesses.) Certainly, we don't need mini-gods prancing around this earth. We do need parents who are crazy about how God made their kids and pointing that out consistently.

One parent I know who is helping his daughter build God-focused confidence is Jeff Henderson, one of the most talented communicators, leaders, and pastors I have ever seen in action. He is the campus pastor of Gwinnett Church (North Point Ministries), and we used to work together at Chick-fil-A. Despite his incredible capabilities, he deflects praise often and makes sure his team and God always get the glory. I wasn't surprised to hear that he'd planned something unusual for his daughter Jessie's thirteenth birthday. He invited about twenty people, mostly adults, who had been pouring into Jessie's life. They took turns affirming

Tips for Kids with a Heart for Humility

- Practice saying, "I'm sorry, I was wrong."
- Acknowledge your weaknesses as often as (or more than) your strengths.
- Praise and lift others up.
- Start a round robin at dinner, with each person naming a gift or strength of the person to his right.
- Take credit for when your team fails.
- Share credit and show grace to the other competitors when your team succeeds.
- Play "I spy humility," and let mom and dad know when you see it.
- Watch for those who deflect praise yet stand tall with confidence.
- Seek to make others successful.
- Plan to do your best and trust God with the rest.
- Practice listening well before sharing your story or opinion.
- Ask someone about her day before you launch into describing yours.

Jessie's character. Affirming how God created her. Praising her for her choices so far. Encouraging her to live out the gifts they already could see in her. What a beautiful way for a dad to champion his daughter while demonstrating quiet confidence in God's story for his family.

I have actually spent a lot of time thinking about this tension between humility and confidence. While I never want my children to think they are superior to others, my hope is to raise confident, strong girls who are passionate about Christ and who lead boldly from their gifts.

The virtue of humility can easily be misunderstood as a charge to train quiet kids who are afraid to speak up for themselves. No way! I don't know about you, but I have no interest in raising doormats or wimps. My goal is to nurture in my kids an assurance of their calling and their gifts. I want them grounded in truth and love so that they can lead well and fulfill God's plan for their lives.

If we err as parents, I hope it will be on the side of affirming and building up our kids' confidence. Our kids need to know we are in their corner. More than that, they need to know Jesus is in their corner, delighting in them. When they have a confidence rooted in His love and ours, they don't need to push themselves into the spotlight.

60 Ways to Bring Out the Giggles

48

Silly Hair Salon.
Give kids squirt bottles, supplies, and freedom to make mom's and dad's hair silly.

I absolutely love this quote from Mark Merrill, founder of All Pro Dad and Family First:

If we think humility is only for wimps and losers, then we really don't know what the word means. Humility can only come from those who actually have something about which to be humble. The humble are those who could crow, but choose not to.[9]

The Christian life often involves going against our natural inclinations and standing against culture. Our kids will share in the desire of their peers to be something, to stand out, to succeed, and to be noticed. These are not bad desires, but as Christians we can approach these desires from a very different perspective. My hope is for my girls to live in a confidence that comes from their identity in Christ, their strength of character, the beauty of their hearts. I want them to stand up boldly for their

49

Air-Guitar Contest. Play a favorite tune and see who can rock the air guitar.

60 Ways to Bring Out the Giggles

beliefs and ideals. However, sometimes their leadership will be shown through humility, service, and gratitude—ultimately an expression of their love for God, not pride of self.

If a child has stellar strength in sports or academics or the arts—in whatever way she stands out beautifully—we can encourage humility by reminding her where that gift came from and who it's meant to point to. And while we cheer our children on in making the most of their God-given skills, let's balance our enthusiasm for their unique gifts with a reminder that their identity is not tied up in what they do but in who they belong to.

My dear friend Kristen stopped me in my tracks the other day when she said of her four-year-old daughter, "I've been praying for Mary Grace this year, for biblical self-esteem." And of course I wanted to know more.

She explained that she is begging God to root that girl's self-esteem and worth in Him. Not in how society, friends, school, or anyone else says she needs to feel. But in how He made her. In His plan for her life. In how He created her to look and in how He designed her for His purposes.

Ah, I just love it! What an amazing prayer for a little girl. For all of us!

As parents, we have an extraordinary opportunity to shape minds and adjust expectations, to create an image of what the end goal looks like for our children. What we promote, celebrate, and hold up as the standard will shape their perception of what matters. If we value only straight As and winning teams, guess what they will spend time doing? If we value perfection on the outside, guess what will be the focus of their hearts, minds, and money?

> **60 Ways to Bring Out the Giggles**
>
> **50**
>
> **Best Mask.** Grab a thick piece of paper and a Popsicle stick for the mask base. Then find anything in the house that can be glued or adhered to a mask. Most creative mask wins.

While arrogance and pride eventually repel others, I believe there are no men more attractive or women more becoming than those who carry themselves with humility, those who are so confident in the love of a Father and secure in their abilities and gifts that they lead with great passion and never worry about taking credit for themselves. These individuals are magnetic! We are drawn to people who are aware of the needs of others and always ready to serve. We are drawn to Christ at work in and through them. His presence creates an internal confidence and beauty that pulls others near to them—and eventually nearer to God.

This is how I hope to challenge and encourage my girls: "I see God's amazing gifts in you, and I trust He will reveal and make them shine in His timing. How can we shine a light on others' gifts in a way that honors God?"

Let's help kids discover their gifts from above. And humbly point them to their heavenly Father as they use their strengths for His glory.

Teaching *Humility*

Be humble, thinking of others as better than yourselves. Don't look out only for your own interests, but take an interest in others, too. *Philippians 2:3–4, NLT*

Virtue Definition for Memorization

Humility: giving God and others center stage

Read in *The Jesus Storybook Bible*

"A giant staircase to heaven," page 48. The tower of Babel, based on Genesis 11.

Questions for Discussion

- Have you ever seen someone celebrate himself or a big win loudly and wildly? How did it make you feel?
- When is it okay to celebrate?
- How would Jesus handle a loss?

- How can you be humble and confident at the same time?
- Where did you get the qualities that make you wonderful?
- How can we use our voices to build up our friends?
- How can we hold our tongues to instill humility and hold back pride?
- Have you ever seen someone share the spotlight? Or hold back a chance to win so that another person is honored?
- What is pride? What are behaviors that make you think someone is prideful? Is it easy to do those things? Can you name two that you can stop doing?
- What's the difference between pride and confidence?

Pray

Lord, You are the absolute picture of humility. When You could have done so much with Your power and might, You chose to serve and give and love in the most humble of circumstances. We want to show others Your love by how we give You the glory for anything in us and in our lives that is good. We pray that we will be the kind of family that consistently lifts up others and is quick to praise others. We want to be confident in You and the strengths You have given us, yet humble before You. We honor You. We love You. Amen.

Activity: Job Well Done

It feels so incredible when your efforts are noticed. This month, your family will practice humility by putting others center stage and giving them that incredible feeling that comes from being appreciated for a job well done.

Supplies

- [ ] Job Well Done postcards (can be downloaded at courtneydefeo.com)
- [ ] crayons
- [ ] cardstock
- [ ] stamps
- [ ] scissors

How This Works

This is your chance to notice and affirm others. Put them center stage and specifically affirm their gifts from above! As you go about your day at school, work, and other activities, keep your eyes peeled for classmates or friends who deserve recognition. It might be the friend who scored the goal. It might be the friend who never scores the goal but always has an incredibly positive attitude.

You are going to create and send to each of these people personalized Job Well Done postcards. Set a goal for yourself to send postcards to eight, ten, or even twenty people this month!

As you write on the postcards, don't forget specifics. Here are a few examples:

- Dear Emma Kate, I noticed how you always include friends. It makes me and all the other girls feel so good. You're such a great friend. I'm thankful for that. Love, Ella
- Dear Mary Virginia, You're really a great tennis player. I noticed how you kept going today in tennis practice after a few tough moments. That's awesome. Great attitude. I'm glad we play together. Love, Ella
- Dear Harper, I noticed how you obey your parents all the time. That reminds me to do the same. Thanks for being my friend. I love you. Larson.
- Dear Annalee, You're a really graceful ballerina. Your twirls are awesome, and you always listen to the teacher. I love when we dance together. I love you. Larson.

Optional Activities

PLAN a night to print your Job Well Done postcards, brainstorm recipients, and personalize the cards.

READ & DISCUSS Proverbs 11:2; 15:33; 22:4; Micah 6:8; James 4:10; 1 Peter 5:5.

ENCOURAGE Think of a time someone in your family demonstrated humility, and share that story at dinner.

11

Gratitude

So Many Reasons
to Be Thankful

Memory Verse for the Month

And whatever you do, whether in word or deed, do it all in the name of the Lord Jesus, giving thanks to God the Father through him. *Colossians 3:17*

It's time you know a little secret about our family. We are absolutely obsessed with Walt Disney World. Obsessed. As a child, I visited Disney World just one time, but my precious husband grew up visiting there regularly, and his adoration for the Magic Kingdom has rubbed off on me. Now we are raising two teacup-riding, Mickey-ear-wearing fans. When we moved to

Orlando, we decided to splurge for the annual passes and let our girls experience the wonder of it all as often as we could.

During one Disney outing on a December Saturday, the girls and I went into one of the sparkling-clean restrooms. I was so glad to see a Disney employee in there so I could finally thank someone in person for those clean restrooms. I looked that beautiful woman in the eyes and genuinely thanked her for how hard she worked. I told her specifically how every time we visit Disney, every restroom is wonderfully clean and always stocked with supplies. I explained the difference this makes for me, as a mom bringing my kids to the park. She absolutely beamed! She proceeded to tell me her name was Ms. Curlie and that she had worked for Disney for twenty-four years. Ella and Larson listened as she described her love for her job and the glass case in her home where she displays special gifts and honors from the company. At the end of our chat, we hugged and Ella snapped a photo of this fun moment. Then we bounced out, waving good-bye to our new friend.

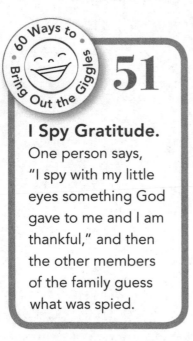

60 Ways to Bring Out the Giggles

51

I Spy Gratitude.
One person says, "I spy with my little eyes something God gave to me and I am thankful," and then the other members of the family guess what was spied.

As we walked away, I said to the girls, "I wish we had something to give her."

My precious Ella immediately said, "Mom, give her my new pin." My heart filled with joy as I dug in my purse for my daughter's brand-new pin she had carefully selected as her memento for the day. She said, "Can I take it to her?"

With a deep sense of pride and love, I said, "You bet, sweetie."

Ella, Larson, and I giggled with joy and ran back to the sparkling restroom. "Merry Christmas!" we declared as Ella presented her gift. Our new friend beamed again and said, "Thank you! This will go in my glass case!"

Ron was waiting nearby holding all our stuff, and he loved hearing about our conversation and the girls' response. That day five hearts were forever sealed with that memory of gratitude. Rather than giving our kids a lecture about being thankful, we all entered together into an experience where gratitude overflowed from truly thankful hearts.

I find it interesting that we didn't mention God's name one time, but we definitely showed His love. My kids felt it in the very depth of their hearts. It was a beautiful moment for me as a mom to think about this glass case that Ella would never see holding a treasure she'd given up to honor someone else.

Fueling Contentment in Our Homes

Ron and I long to see gratitude etched deep in the framework of our home. We have been abundantly blessed throughout our lives, and I never want our girls to take anything for granted. We are forgiven, we have a God who loves and guides us, and we have eternal life. We have food to eat, water to drink, warm beds, clean restrooms, clothes, friends, family—the list goes on and on.

The culture surrounding our kids will tell them daily that they need more. That they aren't enough and they should complain about that. That they need bigger, more, and better. We can create homes that surround them with a different message. We can daily remind them "You are enough" and "God is enough" and "We have enough." By fueling contentment in our families, we can help our children resist the lies of discontent and comparison.

If your home is like mine, most days sound like this: *Can we watch just one more show? Why can't we stop for ice cream? But you never let my friends come over! Why does she always get to choose what we watch? But I want another one!* My biggest frustration is when the discontentment immediately follows a privilege. I've stopped for a treat and they want more. Or I've let them have a friend over for a play date, but it didn't last long enough or they wanted two friends instead of just one. The constant "never enough" mentality can wear me down. The same goes for my husband who, I'm sorry to say, hears the "never enough" chorus from me about our house, decorations, car, clothes, and more. Gratitude is a heart skill I want to arm my kids—and me!—with for life. Are you with me?

Of course, living daily from a place of gratitude is not easy—even for parents. Parenting is a tough job. We have little ones whining and complaining, older ones arguing and resisting. Sometimes it just seems easier to join in the woeful chorus of dissatisfaction. Like a late-spring frost, a layer of discontentment sweeps over our homes and destroys joy before it can burst into bloom. It's a heart-chilling atmosphere for parents and kids alike.

Happily, a touch of gratitude can thaw our hearts and melt away layers of discontentment, complaining, entitlement, and selfish behaviors. So that's what we're going to practice: living each day being thankful to God and showing appreciation of others. Here's our definition for this virtue:

Gratitude: giving thanks and showing heartfelt appreciation

As a mom who wants to nurture contentment in my children, I've learned that I need to first position my own heart in a place of contentment through gratitude. Through my own response to daily life, I can model heartfelt appreciation, teaching my kids how to give thanks to God first, give thanks daily, give thanks specifically, and give thanks during the toughest times. My hope is that, as my family sees my heartfelt appreciation for all the ways God touches my life through them and other people, their own hearts will be warmed and they will become more attuned to gratitude.

Give Thanks to God First

I am a born encourager raised by an encourager. So it's easy for me to see what others are doing well and tell them. My problem is that I often forget to start with the source of all good things: our God! The One who created me, my friends, and my kids and even knows the number of hairs on our heads.

His Word is filled with powerful verses on gratitude and reminders that a heart of thanksgiving starts with our attitude toward Him: "And whatever you do, whether in word or deed, do it all in the name of the Lord Jesus, giving thanks to God the Father through him" (Colossians 3:17).

Even a simple "Thank you, Lord" as we lie down at night or wake up in the morning helps set our minds and hearts in the right

52

60 Ways to Bring Out the Giggles

Photo Album Night. Flip through old pictures, and treasure fun memories.

direction. My friend Emily suggested praying in the car with your kids as you go to school, and we have been trying that lately. I just love it. I've already got them captive, so it's a great time (especially if we started the day on the wrong foot) to refocus our attention on all that is good. If a child is upset about the snack she chose or because her socks feel too itchy, giving thanks to God for all our blessings typically helps us see socks and snack issues from a more reasonable perspective. We also pray for the things that are really on their hearts. Maybe they are worried about a test, excited about a special field trip, or concerned about a friend who is sick. We don't do this every day, but I can tell you that when we do, the day runs more smoothly.

As we strive to model gratitude for our kids, let's consider where the majority of our thankfulness is focused. Are we starting with the source of everything? Are we thanking God for the people He has given us, not just the things? Once we recognize that "every good and perfect gift is from above" (James 1:17), we will see God's hand at work through the people He places in our lives. And we'll be compelled to thank first Him and then His people for all the blessings we enjoy.

Give Thanks Daily

I have never ever met a person who was overly grateful. However, I can name a few who are extremely ungrateful. We just can't overdo thanking God and showing others our heartfelt appreciation.

November offers a great opportunity to focus on the virtue of gratitude, thanks to those precious pilgrims and their choice to pause in appreciation of God's goodness and the generosity of their fellow human beings. However, you certainly can make a practice of thankfulness any month of the year! What does practicing gratitude look like? Keep in mind the two parts of our definition: (1) giving thanks and (2) showing heartfelt appreciation.

We can demonstrate gratitude in how we pray before dinner or before bed. We can give thanks in a less robotic or formulaic style and more

Fun Ways to Grow Hearts of Gratitude

- Praise God through songs; sing and dance together.

- Draw a picture of all God's gifts in your life.

- Put Post-it notes all over the house to thank another family member for specific things.

- Keep a gratitude art journal. Go on a walk, and pick a spot to draw and write. Capture something you see that God has made.

- Keep a box of notes ready to show heartfelt appreciation for others.

- Close each day by thanking God for something big (something He created) and something small (something specific to your life that day).

- At the end of the day, text or e-mail someone who made you feel good and thank the person specifically.

- Take a "Thank You, God" walk as a family, and point out things you appreciate.

- Take the All-Day Grateful Challenge. Make a necklace or bracelet that says grateful, and if you catch yourself complaining, turn it over. Try again the next day to see if you can stay on grateful all day long.

- Call 'em out! Let a supervisor at your local store know you appreciate one of the employees who is doing his job well. Help someone get noticed for doing his best.

sincerely. We might do a round robin before we eat and say, "Name one thing you want to thank God for today."

And we can demonstrate genuine appreciation simply by teaching our kids to make eye contact with their teachers and say thanks before leaving class. Or they might slip a quick note of thanks into a friend's book bag. We might show gratitude in the way we thank our kids for something they did around the house. It means so much to them when we notice their efforts and take time to tell them how much we value their help. Each tiny deposit of gratitude we make in someone else's heart can make an incredibly big difference in that person's outlook.

60 Ways to Bring Out the Giggles

53

Best Bath Hair.
If siblings bathe together, let them take turns making Mohawks and other funny hairstyles.

What do my children hear most often from me? Do they hear me thanking their daddy for working so hard? Or publicly thanking their teacher for how she cares for my kids? Or telling my mom that I'm grateful for her? Are my words to the girls filled with criticism, or do I catch them doing things right and tell them how incredibly pleased I am when they make wise choices and do the right thing? When I affirm my family, I see their souls light up. I see it in their body language and their smiles.

And when it comes to God, am I grateful and have I given Him proper thanks for all the good things already surrounding me, or am I too focused on begging Him for progress and favors? I want my girls to feel God's love for and approval of them through me. I want gratitude to flow from the abundance in my life. I want to be looking for God working in my girls and be ready to praise Him.

This is the privilege of parenting with God's love and grace on our side. We have so much to share that we cannot claim as our own.

Give Thanks Specifically

When we moved next door to the Werner family, we honestly knew these neighbors were a gift from above. Of all the streets, neighborhoods, and houses, how did we land next door to Linda Werner? This woman has become another mother, a mentor, and a dear friend.

During the past year, the year of her sixtieth birthday, Linda has been on a gratitude journey that has been incredibly powerful to witness. She took the year off from her teaching and mentoring ministry and has been flying all around the country to thank the people who had the most impact on her life. Linda is making an effort to thank each individual— from Dr. James Dobson to Bill Hybels to the woman who led her to Christ—face to face.

The most beautiful thing she does is write a letter detailing the specific things this person did or said that brought something good to Linda's life. She reads the letter before giving it to the recipient. She told me that one highly esteemed leader and speaker had tears streaming down his face as she read his letter. He was immeasurably touched to realize the effect

54

60 Ways to Bring Out the Giggles

Pillow Fight. Grab some pillows and go to war in a big open room. (Heads are off limits.)

his words had on her. One author thought Linda must be terminally ill to do something so remarkable.

Linda is not ill. She is simply obeying God. She doesn't really have time or money to do all this, but she's making it happen because God prompted her to do so. Can you imagine the impact she is having on those who so deeply affected her? Hearing her stories inspired me to write a heartfelt e-mail to my first public-relations professor and thank him for believing in me.

Gratitude means so much more when we get specific. Think of the difference it makes when your husband says "I love how you roasted those vegetables" instead of "Dinner is good, honey." Both are expressions of appreciation, but a bit of added detail confirms that the words are truly heartfelt.

Ron can leave off giving me gifts for life if he'll just write me a note describing specifically why he loves me and what he sees in me. Those words are jet fuel for the soul. When my kids tell me specifically why I'm their favorite mom, my heart fills up. When a fan of my blog takes the time to share specifically how a particular blog post shaped her thinking as a mom, I am encouraged.

Showing heartfelt appreciation through a specific expression of thanks requires time, intentionality, and practice. When my girls were tiny, it felt like torture just getting them to say "thank you" to someone before we left their home. We are now moving into specifics. We say "Thank you for my dinner!" to someone at every restaurant before we leave. Or "Thank you for having us over" before we leave a friend's home. We do our best to be specific in thank-you notes. In fact, I would like to make a motion for all of us to use blank cards and just write exactly what's on our hearts. Those words of appreciation will feed the recipients' souls.

In a similar way, being specific when we thank our Lord has a way of feeding our own souls, as we absorb the truth of how blessed we are. Instead of asking our girls to simply say "Thank you for this day," we encourage them to thank God for particular events and things, and have fun filling in the blank with colorful detail: "Thank You for _____."

We even did that on a hike one time, really loud, and they loved it. "Thank You for…pine cones, Lord! Thank You for…birds, Lord! Thank You for…the blue sky, Lord!"

Give Thanks During the Toughest Times

With real life come real problems. Miscarriages, deaths, bullying, friend drama, disabilities, and financial troubles. How can we lead our kids to live with hearts of gratitude even in their toughest seasons? By helping them find reasons to give thanks anyway.

Ella is not a big fan of wearing glasses. However, this one thing in her life has allowed us some great discussions around gratitude. Together we thank God for eyes that see. We thank God for glasses that help us to see

Catch Phrases for **Gratitude**

- Thank You, God, for… ("I spy" game)
- Gratitude is giving thanks and showing heartfelt appreciation.
- Gratitude increases contentment.
- Instead of wanting more, let's be thankful for what we have.
- We have so many reasons to be thankful.
- Some of the people in our lives are God's greatest gifts to us.
- You get what you get, and you don't throw a fit.

better. We thank God for all our other body parts that work. Gratitude doesn't make her struggle disappear, but it gives her a broader perspective. I love Ann Voskamp's observation: "Perspective can always adopt gratitude—and gratitude always parents joy."[10]

The reality is that our families will inevitably travel through small struggles and big ones. How we handle and respond to the small struggles will likely be how we handle the big ones. Will we point our kids to Christ and assure them He is good even when life is bad? Will we still praise Him in the face of broken air conditioners and sick dogs and housing moves?

55

Balloon Hair. Grab a balloon and rub it on a child's head for frizzy, funny hair and instant giggles.

God doesn't ask us to praise Him just when jobs are paying and kids are soaring. He calls us to give thanks even in the midst of the worst times. The apostle Paul reminds us that we are to "give thanks in all circumstances; for this is God's will for you in Christ Jesus" (1 Thessalonians 5:18).

We have certainly had struggles in our family, but I cannot fathom the depth of pain some of our friends have faced. I have watched as my friends have put Paul's words into practice, and God has honored their dependence on Him. They have gained perspective and strength by choosing to thank and praise Him in the midst of their hard times.

If you or your child is facing pain or disappointment right now, I believe in the bottom of my heart that God loves you and He will use your pain for a purpose. I'm confident that if you can practice gratitude in the midst of your worst times, your kids will look back on this season and remember God's strength and faithfulness.

Gratitude Is a Mind Trick

Do you believe gratitude comes from the heart or the mind? I actually believe it's both. We can cultivate a heart of gratitude by training our minds to think on the very things that bring us contentment: "Finally, brothers and sisters, whatever is true, whatever is noble, whatever is right, whatever is pure, whatever is lovely, whatever is admirable—if anything is excellent or praiseworthy—think about such things" (Philippians 4:8).

If we look closely, each of us will realize that our lives are filled with goodness. Even in the midst of the very worst circumstances, goodness exists. God is never far and we are never alone.

As a mom, I'd rather not spend my days pointing out the ungrateful ways and bad behavior of my children. Instead I aim to make our home a place of gratitude, a place where we continue to point our minds and hearts toward the things that are pure and lovely.

Every day I need to examine my Facebook feed, the words of my mouth, statements of my Twitter account, and conversations with my kids to be sure I'm pointing to abundance, not scarcity. I've been known to complain about the too-hot days or crowds of Florida. I know what you're thinking, *Um, have you noticed you're living in the sunniest, happiest place? Alrighty then, sister. Zip it!* You're exactly right.

When we make a practice of noticing and delighting in the goodness all around us, we will have a different perspective toward that husband who left his towel on the bathroom floor and the kids who left something nasty in the sink. As we revel in the abundance of God's love and blessings, we cannot help but be grateful. And it will become the habit of our families to express specific heartfelt appreciation and give thanks to Him daily, no matter what.

Teaching Gratitude

And whatever you do, whether in word or deed, do it all in the name of the Lord Jesus, giving thanks to God the Father through him. *Colossians 3:17*

Virtue Definition for Memorization

Gratitude: giving thanks and showing heartfelt appreciation

Read in *The Jesus Storybook Bible*

"The singer," page 228. The Sermon on the Mount, based on Matthew 6; 9; and Luke 12.

Questions for Discussion

- Think of someone you know who is a grateful person. How can you tell?
- What are some signs that someone has an ungrateful heart?
- Have we been given much or little?
- What things could we do as a family to show our gratitude to God?

- Should we praise God during times of plenty or all the time?
- What does comparison do to our hearts of gratitude?
- How can we be more intentional about showing gratitude for the people in our lives?
- God hasn't just given us things; He's blessed us with people too! Count your blessings, all of them!

Pray

Dear Lord, we come before You humbled today by the many blessings You have given to our family. We thank You for the gift of Your Son and the gift of eternal life. We know we don't deserve any of Your gifts, and we pray that our grateful hearts will help others see You in us. Please take away any greed or envy that settles in us. Help us be the first to celebrate others and thank them genuinely. We are so very thankful for every single thing and person You have placed in our lives. You are worthy of all our praise. Amen.

Activity: Give Thanks Bag

Sometimes the very best way to solve discontentment is to open your eyes to the blessings right in front of you. This month we are going to let each child enjoy the fun of sharing. They will get a chance to choose things that are special to them, then present their blessings to the family and tell why they are thankful. Counting our blessings together breeds contentment and nurtures hearts of gratitude.

Supplies

☐ one tote bag (more, if you want one for each family member)

☐ markers or fabric iron-on letters

☐ timer

How This Works

As a family, make a Give Thanks bag out of a spare canvas tote or one you buy at a craft store. You can make one per child or just use one for the entire family. Write *Give Thanks* on the bag with a marker or use fabric iron-on letters. Use your imagination and let the kids get creative to make this a fun and memorable bag.

Every Sunday this month, children will each place in the Give Thanks bag five things around the house they want to thank God for. Encourage them to think beyond the "things" and include people or experiences, perhaps through photos or other mementos. Then they'll show the family what they collected and explain specifically why they're thankful for each item.

After each child (adults can participate too) has shared the five items for which she is thankful, it's time for round 2! Again each child will fill the bag with five items, this time with the intention of donating those items to a friend or ministry in need. The group or individual recipient can vary each week. Brainstorm together as a family to identify a friend, ministry, or organization that can use the items collected.

Optional Activities

PLAN a night to treat a friend or family member to an expression of your appreciation, perhaps an ice-cream date or dinner out. Surprise someone who hardly ever gets recognized.

READ & DISCUSS Psalm 107:1; Matthew 6:21; Ephesians 1:16–18; Colossians 3:16; 1 Thessalonians 5:18.

ENCOURAGE Identify three people who have inspired your family, and send them personalized notes of gratitude.

12

Generosity

Join in the Adventure of Giving

Memory Verse for the Month

Command them to do good, to be rich in good deeds, and to be generous and willing to share.

1 Timothy 6:18

Have you ever eaten a sub sandwich with mayonnaise and cheese, no meat? Me neither. But that's what my brother, Drew, wanted every day, and he was a serious athlete growing up, so my mom took him to the sub shop often. Mom, who can talk to anyone, soon made friends with the kind sub lady, who after a few visits had his delightful order going even before my mom and Drew got out of the car.

One afternoon when they stopped by, they had to wait because their favorite sandwich maker was on the phone, clearly flustered and upset. Overhearing bits and pieces of the phone call, Mom realized that their sub friend needed to fix her car, but the bill was much more than she could afford. Mom got an idea. She raced home to drop off Drew and his cheese-and-mayo delight, and I got wrangled into the adventure. Mom and I drove to the bank and got some cash. She put it in a plain envelope and marked a sweet message on the outside to make clear who the package was for while keeping the giver anonymous. We parked far enough away that she wouldn't spot the familiar car and recognize Mom, then I delivered the great news and scampered off before she could say anything. All I got to see on my way out was her look of confusion and surprise, but I imagined her tears. I ran to the car, Mom smiled, and we drove off.

60 Ways to Bring Out the Giggles

56

Nursery-Rhyme Time. Hum a nursery rhyme and ask the family to guess it.

This wasn't the only time Mom did something like this. Generosity was a core virtue in my childhood home. Our parents held material things with open hands. They were always on the lookout for ways to help others with our time, talents, or resources. They donated clothes, hosted parties, made meals for those in need, sent support and sponsor checks for years to more organizations than I'll ever know, and faithfully tithed. Observing it all, I couldn't help but see the joy in their hearts.

So I was thrilled to be invited that day into the conspiracy of giving generously. That one gift left a mark on the sandwich lady, but my parents' lifetime of generous giving left a mark on me. That's why all these years later I'm on the lookout for opportunities to invite my girls along on similar surprise adventures. It's just so fun to be a light in the world, to remind folks that they are loved and cared for. If we can help, we will. In small ways and big ways.

One of my top goals as a parent is to raise my girls so they yearn to give to others, not just shop for themselves. So I spend a lot of time considering how I can show them the beauty of generosity, how it delights another's soul and feeds our own. How can I help them recognize the distinction between needs and wants? How do I help them experience generosity in a way that overflows from an abundance of God's love and grace? I pray daily that God will etch generosity so deep in their hearts that even when they have little to give, they are first to step up.

Holding Everything with Open Hands

As with all the virtues, it is imperative that we define generosity for our kids. Big words are cute when they try to pronounce them but not very effective at shaping hearts. Kids need tangible concepts to grab hold of. So here's our definition for this virtue:

Generosity: giving what we have so others feel God's love

Here's how I've explained it in our home: "Girls, what does generosity mean? It means giving what we have so others feel God's love. What can we give? Anything! Our toys, our energy, our time, our money—whatever God asks us to give so that other people feel joy and kindness and love. And so they'll see God in us. How can we be generous today? Is there someone who comes to your mind?"

Wherever we may live, most of us don't have to look far beyond our front porches to find someone with a genuine need. I know that not far from my home are people who need pants, a house, a new leg, love. They need Jesus. And God has given us the privilege of helping to meet those needs.

When we set out to bless others—from garbage collectors to the homeless to school teachers—something unexpected happens: our own perspectives are transformed. Our hearts are changed as we see the very love of Christ flow through us to others. Our families are changed as pure kindness and love bubble up and out of our children. Generosity is addictive and contagious; we want to repeat and share the experience.

What a difference it makes when we realize that God has blessed us so much because He wants us to have the privilege of blessing others! Will we be faithful with all He has given us? This is a constant prayer in my life. I want to be faithful with our money, our house, my few blog readers, one book, two kids—so that if God chooses to expand my influence, I will be ready. I want Him to know He can trust me to give and hold everything with open hands. All I have—time, resources, material things—belongs to Him.

My precious friend Ashley continues to amaze me with her generous spirit. One day she was carrying a designer Kate Spade purse, a gift from her mother, when another woman commented how much she liked it. Ashley felt a nudge in her spirit and, without hesitation, joyfully handed it over to the stranger. Are you shocked? The lady was too. But Ashley knows that our stuff is just temporal. Imagine how we could shock the world if we and our kids follow her example of showing God's love and glory everywhere we go!

Lighting Up Our World

During the time both my girls were born, we were living in Atlanta and attending Buckhead Church. My desire to give and serve increased exponentially as we got involved in the church and with North Point Ministries. Andy Stanley and Jeff Henderson had such a unique way of alerting the church to the needs of a city without paralyzing us with guilt. Their enthusiasm made us feel needed, that we matter in the story of God's kingdom. They reminded us of God's plan for the church and how we are to intersect with the lives of individuals all over our communities. We were inspired regularly to love our neighbors and meet their needs, from the basics to the big stuff. They also made us aware of the importance of not simply writing checks but actually getting our hands dirty, drawing close enough to look individuals in the face and connect with them on a personal level.

Their words stirred my heart to start something huge, to put my creativity to work in meeting needs. In addition, as I sat and talked with

Catch Phrases for **Generosity**

- It is truly better to give than receive.
- Don't worry about what you're getting this Christmas. Your mom and dad will always have something special for you.
- Let's stay focused on how our family can give generously.
- Since "everything we have is for Him," let's use it!
- How fun to take what God has already given us and think how we can bless others with it.
- God loves a cheerful giver.

others in small-group sessions, we would all get so excited about the idea of serving together with our precious kids. We wanted them to experience the joy of practicing generosity from an early age. But as we looked for opportunities to get them involved, we kept hitting walls and limits on what they were allowed to do because of their age.

Around this same time, I learned about Robyn, the founder of The Birthday Project. This project involves carrying out a number of random acts of kindness that correspond to the number of years she's celebrating at each birthday. Her approach stuck in my head and heart. How selfless! How amazing.

All this stuff was percolating in my brain and heart—the desire to give, the hope of teaching generosity to my kids, the excitement about random acts of kindness—and the result was a pretty exciting idea called Light 'Em Up.

60 Ways to Bring Out the Giggles

57

Karaoke Contest. Categories might include best Disney movie song, best slow song, best oldies song.

The core idea was to use the month of December to help our kids experience generosity. Instead of focusing on what they would be getting for Christmas, they would be focusing on what they could be doing for others. On December 25 we celebrate the arrival of Jesus, the biggest gift of all, and what better gift can we give Him in return than to love on and serve His people? With this in mind, I challenged the readers of my blog to join me in turning the tables from *getting* to *giving*. Together we launched a Light 'Em Up campaign for families to experience generosity together, to make a difference in the lives of people in their community through random acts of kindness. The goal was to empower families to believe that no matter their age, our kids can be used for a purpose and learn a critical virtue in the process. That blog post went live on November 27, 2011. Just four days later thousands of people had visited the site to download the free ideas and gift tags, and get started lighting up their world.

Since then the idea has been pinned more than 140,000 times on Pinterest, and over 150 women have committed to leading groups, from high school kids to classrooms to moms' groups, to light up their communities. From Ukraine to Australia to California, moms are fired up about bringing generosity to life in the hearts of their kids. And giving God the glory. I am so eternally grateful for all those who keep sharing this idea. I believe we will never know on this side of eternity the impact our families have had for Jesus.

The most exciting part? Kids' hearts are changing. Jeremiah caught the Light 'Em Up bug and decided he wanted to do it wherever and whenever. While on vacation he asked his parents if he could leave a note of thanks for the people who cleaned their room—all his idea. *Keep it going, Jeremiah!* Cate and Sophia can be seen blazing through our downtown at Christmas time, leaving candy canes everywhere. They fly in and out of stores with the biggest smiles and light up the entire community. They now can "light up" a Publix in minutes flat without any help from their parents. These two also left donuts and orange juice for their garbagemen. The joy on their faces is contagious. Sara Easley, a blog follower and mom of two, told me her kids love the idea of Light 'Em Up so much

58

60 Ways to Bring Out the Giggles

Makeovers. Let kids do mom's makeup.

that they did one act of kindness every day leading up to Lent and then again for Mother's Day. These are just a few examples of the kids whose hearts have been captured by the experience of being used to show others the light and love of God.

In the activity at the end of this chapter, I'll tell you more about how you can Light 'Em Up this Christmas season or any other time of the year. We've now done this program during the summer and for Mother's Day, and it really works great anytime of the year. Generosity lights up the hearts of others.

The Cheerful (and Not So Cheerful) Giver

One of the secrets generous people know is that giving benefits the giver as much as, if not more than, the receiver. In fact, Paul urges us in Acts 20:35, to "remember the words of the Lord Jesus, that He Himself said, 'It is more blessed to give than to receive'" (NASB). But how many of us live as if we really believe that? It's certainly not an easy concept to persuade our children to believe when they're arguing about who gets the bigger slice of cake.

As delighted as I've been about the response to our Light 'Em Up campaign, I know kids don't always get fully on board. You might hand a candy cane to your toddler so he can pass it on to the store clerk to brighten her day. Instead he declares incredibly loudly so all of the town can hear, "No! I don't want to give that! I want to eat it!" Not exactly how you had envisioned your morning of honoring God through giving.

We have certainly had our share of Light 'Em Up trips when, for whatever reason, a child was not in the mood. She might have been feeling grumpy or too shy to go in the fire station, or she simply wouldn't hand over the flower. It's not that my kids were being defiant on such occasions; they just didn't have happy, generous hearts 100 percent of the time. And that was okay. Instead of abandoning the plan, we just let the reluctant child walk beside us as we continued on. No one was forced to speak or act; they simply were present for the activity. We certainly talked about the purpose of our trips before, during, and after. And they got it.

The fact is, at times our kids will be reluctant givers. Our job is to keep practicing and praying that God will help them learn to live with open hands, as He instructs: "Give generously to them and do so without a grudging heart; then because of this the LORD your God will bless you in all your work and in everything you put your hand to" (Deuteronomy 15:10).

If your children resist your efforts to help them learn generosity, I encourage you to be patient. They are still watching and they will come around. Our goal in this book is to teach virtues through fun activities, but no one will be giggling if we are yelling about a child's lack of cooperation. Bringing discipline into the situation may actually undermine your efforts. "Be generous" is not an order to be shouted but a principle to grow into. And they will get there eventually as they experience for themselves the joy of giving.

You know the wretched feeling of failure that comes when one of your kids shouts "No! Mine!" and curls away from a friend with a death grip on the object of their

59

Secret Pal.
Slip a small gift under a family member's pillow or into her backpack, and see how long it takes her to notice.

60 Ways to Bring Out the Giggles

mutual affection. I know that feeling. I've seen my kids do it, and I've caught myself responding, though less obviously, with the same greedy attitude. It lurks in us all.

The opposite feeling comes from a heart filled with gratitude and contentment. When you see it happening, your heart will feel as if it's about to combust. Your little one will say to a friend, "Sure! You can take it. Sure! You can borrow it. Sure! You can take a turn." And I want you to do a happy dance right then and there because the tide is turning. Young hearts are shifting.

But learning generosity takes time, so we have to pray and prepare ourselves for the process. And I'm convinced our perseverance will pay off. One of my most favorite moments as a parent took place on a day we went through the Dollar Tree store and scattered bags in which we'd tucked a dollar plus tax and a note that said, "Surprise! Our family believes it is better to give than receive. Enjoy this treat." Larson, Ella, one of Ella's school buddies, and I hid these bags all over the store. After twenty minutes or so of hiding bags and giggling, we jetted out and jumped in the car.

60 Gift-Wrap Challenge. Pick several awkwardly shaped items and see who can do the best job gift-wrapping them in newspaper.

As we were driving away, a woman tapped on my window and asked if she could wash my window for spare change. I had just left literally every dollar and cent of my cash in that store. I apologized, said no, and was driving off when Ella said, "Mom, tell her about the money!" Beaming with pride that her heart was prompted to do that, I put the car in reverse, returned to the woman, and told her about our little secret. Her eyes lit up and our hearts lit up as we watched her walk inside on a hunt for dollars.

When it comes to carrying out acts of generosity, my strongest recommendation is to let your kids lead. As 2 Corinthians 9:7 reminds us, "Each of you should give what you have decided in your heart to give, not reluctantly or under compulsion, for God loves a cheerful giver." Put a jar in the house, fill it with their ideas, and let them choose what excites them. When they are told how to love others, it feels forced; but I'm convinced that when they get to initiate the love, you'll see their hearts change.

Let Your Hearts and God Lead the Way

For those of us who love Jesus, generosity can—and should—become a natural part of daily life, much like service. But at some point our financial resources will run out, along with our time and energy. We can be overwhelmed by the sheer number of needs around the world and the lack of resources. On any given day we might receive several fund-raising letters, hear about a family in need, pass someone on the road with a sign declaring his need, read about a building campaign on Facebook—and end up discouraged and exhausted. Personally I would love to solve everything, including world peace, by next weekend. So I have appreciated the friends and mentors who teach me how to give cheerfully yet wisely, recognizing we all have limited resources and time.

The best part is that God knows our hearts. There is no "right way" or certain way to give. He does have a few things to say in the Bible about tithing, but He makes it clear that giving is not about the number of zeros on the check but about the state of our hearts. So I try not to get hung up on too many details. Does that party I threw for the lady at the church count as giving? Is that tax deductible? Is that gift for my ministry leader part of my tithe? Rather than worrying about how to measure my giving, I want my heart to be pure. I want my girls to learn that a giving heart simply involves a willingness to take what we have and use it for others so they feel God's love.

Sometimes what we have is not very much. Or it may be that we're low on money but have plenty of time, or the other way around. That's where God comes in. It's a good idea to ask Him for clarity: *Where do You want our family to focus? What is our mission as a family?* The answer will often be in line with the passions and gifts He has already laid in your hearts. Terrific synergy can happen when a family starts giving, serving, and loving together. For example, if God has called your family to love orphans, various aspects of your lives will all line up so you can do so. In our family, in this season, God has called us to empower moms and change little lives. Our time, resources, and talents are all headed that way right now. As the girls grow I want to be sensitive to where God is leading them to serve. He will make that clear, and I can't wait to cheer them on.

Teaching Generosity

Command them to do good, to be rich in good deeds, and to be generous and willing to share. *1 Timothy 6:18*

Virtue Definition for Memorization

Generosity: giving what we have so others feel God's love

Read in *The Jesus Storybook Bible*

"The King of all kings," page 192. The story of the three wise men based on Matthew 2.

Questions for Discussion

- Who serves our family most often during our errands and day-to-day activities?
- Who are the most selfless workers in our community?
- Does our family have a passion for a particular ministry or group of people in our town?
- Which of our neighbors could use an extra hand?

- What are some big ways we could surprise some people with generosity?
- Today, to whom can we give, even in some small way?

Pray

Lord, we want You to be known and Your will to be done. We want to give You glory through our giving. We have so much to offer others and our community—our time, our talents, our smiles, and our ideas. Let us be quick to hear and obey Your prompting. Help us give to Your children and let them feel Your love in a brand-new way. From the tiniest gifts to outrageous gifts, we are ready for whatever You have for our family. We ask You to use us to light up the lives of others, to light up our community in a way that brings You glory. Go before us and show us where to go. Amen.

Activity: Light 'Em Up

Brace yourselves for a beautiful transformation and a new tradition that honors our precious Savior born on Christmas Day. I can't think of better gift to give Him than giving generously each and every day. Shall we do this? Are you in? I am certainly excited for the people you will bless with your generosity, but I am most excited for the work Light 'Em Up will do in the hearts of your family as they experience the joy of serving others.

Supplies

You can accomplish the spirit of this task by simply buying a few boxes of candy canes or baking some cookies, and using the printable tags at courtneydefeo.com or making homemade cards. Small gestures go a long way toward lifting the spirits of others.

However, you may feel called to surprise some families and individuals in unique ways. If so, go for it! Big ideas range from paying off someone else's layaway gifts to paying another table's restaurant bill. Go as wild and crazy as God leads you!

How This Works

Little kids to teens can engage in and find meaningful moments with the family. This is certainly an appropriate activity during the month of December; it will keep your children focused on the reason for the season, on giving rather than getting. However, generosity is a part of loving others and following Christ all year long. So whenever you choose, dedicate one month to serving others in your community. Your family can choose how to customize the plan for age-specific activities. Anyone old enough to walk and talk can begin practicing generosity by making cards and handing out candy canes. This and other small random acts of kindness suggested below have worked well for many other families.

Here are some specific ideas to stir up creative acts of generosity:

- Pay someone's toll.
- Clean up an elderly neighbor's yard.
- Thank your local firefighters with a heartfelt note and treat.

- Leave an encouraging message using sidewalk chalk on your neighbor's driveway.
- Tape a *large* sign on top of your trash can with a little treat for your garbage collector.
- Tape money with a note to a vending machine.
- Tuck money in the toy section of any store with a little note for one happy boy or girl.
- Have your child write a note to a friend telling her why she is special.
- Take coffee or cocoa to someone who works in the cold.
- Feed someone who is hungry.
- Buy a bunch of flowers, and give them away one at a time, as prompted.
- Buy someone's meal at a restaurant.
- Thank your police officers with a heartfelt note and treat.
- Thank a librarian and hide some money in the books while you are there.
- Make a meal for a family that could use an extra hand.
- Find out what your local children's hospitals will allow and go spread love.
- Find an assisted-living home, and see how you can spread some cheer with your little ones.
- Set up a free hot-cocoa stand for a group that could really use it.
- Sweep a neighbor's porch and driveway.
- Wrap gifts for a neighbor or friend.
- Tape quarters to bubblegum machines.
- Take candy canes and simple notes to thank the mall employees working Christmas week.
- Sneak in a friend's house and clean it.

- Thank your church staff, teachers, volunteers, and pastor.
- Go on a scavenger hunt for change in your home, and drop it in the local Salvation Army bucket.
- Buy lunch for the car behind you in a drive-through.
- Take a few minutes to hold the door for everyone walking into an office or store.
- Take a treat to the janitors at your child's school or church.
- Bring a treat to your teacher with a note saying specifically why you appreciate him.

You'll find more resources at courtneydefeo.com, including gift tags to make it really easy to leave surprise treats and run! Strangers or loved ones—whomever you choose to light up—will be left with a touching message that explains your sweet act of generosity. The site also provides a planning document for organizing your family's Light 'Em Up campaign and more.

Optional Activities

PLAN a night to review all the Light 'Em Up printables and free materials, and plan your approach.

READ & DISCUSS Matthew 25:21; Acts 20:35; 1 Timothy 6:18–19; 1 John 3:17.

ENCOURAGE Buy a pack of Post-it notes, and leave a note on your child's mirror every time you notice him carry out a generous act. Affirm your family all month long!

A Closing Letter of Grace

At the close of every day, every school event, every parenting book I read, I find myself comparing. *Am I good enough? Do I have what it takes?* I suspect that's a natural part of being a passionate, intentional mom.

If you've made it this far in reading my book, I know a few things about you: You are madly in love with your kids. You want the best for them. And you do not want to mess up. I know this is true for you, because I know it's true for me.

When I was growing up, my mom kept a substantial cereal stash that made our house the place to be. If you said you loved Trix, my mom had a box of it waiting in the cabinet for the next time you came. If you spent the night at our house and mentioned your preference for Froot Loops, then Toucan Sam appeared in the lineup.

Mom's cereal stash was legendary, a perfect example of the way she showed love in our home. Every child—not just her own kids, but every child who entered her door—was noticed and heard. My mom wasn't perfect. Just like me, she sometimes lost her temper, she overreacted, and she messed up. She is human. However, she is filled to overflowing with a love that covered everything in our home like magic pixie dust. She loves Jesus and wants others to know Him and experience His love. My friends felt this over the years, and they still run back to her home for the occasional Meese hug, song, or meal.

This is the goal of all our "virtuous" efforts: reflecting the heart of our heavenly Father within the walls of our home. The way we talk, the way we forgive, the way we give—every action is a chance to show His grace and love. I don't want to be Jesus for my kids; I just want to draw them close to Him. I don't need to be perfect, because He already is. My friend and author Jeannie Cunnion has encouraged me greatly with her journey of grace in parenting through *Parenting the Wholehearted Child*. She wrote, "I was focused on teaching my kids what they had to do for Jesus rather than teaching them what Jesus has already done for them through his death on the cross and his resurrection."[11]

I have to remind myself daily that God offers grace. Yes, we are going to mess up. We will not, cannot, get all this parenting stuff just right. But God fills in the gaps and gives us tremendous grace and mercy along the road. I hope you've heard that loud and clear throughout these pages.

Actually, I'm thankful there is no road map, recipe book, or perfect plan for parenting; if there were, I'd be tempted to think I didn't need Jesus. Being a mom has driven me to Him more often than ever before in my life, desperate for discernment, wisdom, comfort, guidance, and love.

Dependence on Him is a good thing. We were never meant to travel this road alone, and He knows the best way. So I hope you will be inspired and motivated by this book, but please don't take your direct cues from me or anything other than God and His Word.

The Gift of a Legacy

Flip through a few baby photos, and you'll be reminded just how quickly these years are flying past. That's why I'm convinced it's so important to be intentional in our parenting. The effects of our choices will echo through our children's lives and for generations to come.

Not long ago, when wading through a sea of e-mails, I found one with the subject line "MRS. KIRBY (your grandmother)." This came as quite a surprise for two reasons: first, because my grandmother had passed away several months earlier, and second, because this e-mail came through my website contact section, which meant a stranger was writing to me about my family.

I was blown away to discover why this person had taken the time to contact me. She had bought my grandmother's house and hoped to raise her family in it for years to come. In talking with folks around town, she had learned about my grandmother's legacy of faith, how she'd made serving God the priority of her life. She found some old papers that reinforced what she'd heard. As a Christian mom, she was so excited to think that she too could carry on in that same home the legacy of faith begun by my grandmother.

As one of twenty-five grandchildren, I didn't receive very many mementos after my grandmother passed away. Reading this e-mail was like opening a treasured keepsake. The story kept going. This woman revealed that she'd found some items left behind, along with those old papers. Though she wanted to keep the items, she prayed and felt God nudging her. So she started researching and found one of my online blog posts that described how much I loved my grandmother and how I loved her faith. Her legacy. And this woman knew I should have the papers and items she had found. As I read the e-mail, I sobbed. Oh, how I missed her. And I was so thankful for this woman, that she took the time to give me this gift. This little wink from God.

I was also reminded how simple passing on faith can be. My grandmother didn't have a blog, a business, a ministry, or anything you'd ever know about on Facebook. She simply loved her family and she loved Jesus, and she told everyone she knew about Him. She prayed every day for all of us. Our family has a deep heritage of faith, and we are committed to carrying it forward through the generations.

Everything we've talked about in this book, everything I do with my girls at home is meant to reinforce the one truth I want my kids to know and the one hope I have for their lives: I want them to know the love of Jesus for themselves, and I hope they'll share it with everyone they meet.

Here's my heart's desire in a nutshell:

The DeFeo Family
In this house, we will love others
in a way that lights up the world.
(And we will giggle, often.)

I am praying for you as you join me on this journey. Come with me and let's show them His love.

Acknowledgments

I keep in touch with most people I have ever met from elementary school (Hey, Miss Cantrell!) to high school (What's up, Cara!) to my mail carrier (You're my buddy, Casey!) to my favorite dining-room hostess at Chick-fil-A (You're family, Miss Brenda!). So it is quite impossible to properly acknowledge all the people who have influenced my life or inspired this book. For each of you, I say a heartfelt "Thank you!" This opportunity is more than I deserve, and I consider it an honor to share how virtues, love, and laughter can impact the heartbeat of your home.

To my precious parents: Thank you for teaching me to love above all else, for your unconditional support, for your belief in me, and for rooting me in the firm foundation of Jesus Christ. For creating a home I can use as a model for my own.

To my sweet siblings: My favorite place to giggle is on Mom and Dad's porch with you by my side. I adore you.

To my in-laws: Thank you for loving me like I'm your own and raising one amazing son.

To the Lil Light O' Mine fans and friends: Without you, this would not be happening. You bought the ABC Scripture Cards, you shared blog posts, and you gave me courage and confidence. Thank you for allowing me to share ideas for our families and for making them better! I love our community, and I do believe our kids can light up the world. We are in this together.

To my dear friends: I just can't name all of you, but you know who you are. We've changed diapers, we've cried over coffee, we've texted verses, we've asked tough questions, we've prayed for our kids, and we've discussed every bit of this book. You are my focus group, my editors, my constant affirmation, my cheerleading team, and the strongest women I know. "Thank you" will never be enough. Your hearts, prayers, edits, and words are in every page. Your families are the very best examples of real faith, lived out in the mess and the beautiful moments of life.

To the prayer team behind this book: Thank you for knowing my heart to impact families and honor God.

To Casey Darnell: You aren't just the songwriter of "In This House," you are a treasured friend. I will be forever grateful for how you put my heart to music. I can see families dancing now.

To the team that made this book possible: Behind this author is just an insecure girl who dreams big and loves God bigger. Thanks for pushing me beyond what I thought was possible. Keep investing in people. Your words stick. Robert and Bobbie Wolgemuth, Austin Wilson, Laura Barker, Katie Douglas, Lysa TerKeurst and the whole Proverbs 31 and She Speaks team, Kay Wyma, Jeff Henderson, David Salyers, Lisa Churchfield, Regina Williams, and the entire WaterBrook Multnomah team.

And to my incredible family: For the months my face was in my computer so that others might know the God we love so much. You make my heart literally leap, all three of you. Your sacrifices will touch so many lives. I am proud to call you mine.

To my heavenly Father: Every bit of this is so that my family and others will see a reflection of You. I can only imagine the overwhelming joy we will feel in Your presence, in Your house, one day. I do believe giggles will erupt. With all my heart and desire, this is to honor and glorify You.

Notes

1. Robert Wolgemuth, *The Most Important Place on Earth* (Nashville: Thomas Nelson, 2004), 136.
2. Kay Warren, *Choose Joy: Because Happiness Isn't Enough* (Grand Rapids: Revell, 2012), 32.
3. John Piper, *The Pleasures of God* (Colorado Springs: Multnomah, 2012), 282.
4. Lewis B. Smedes, *Forgive and Forget* (New York: HarperCollins, 1996), 133.
5. For a fun song written especially for this book, be sure to check out "In This House" by Casey Darnell (available on iTunes).
6. Sandra Stanley, "Courage for Teens," blog post on courtneydefeo.com, January 22, 2014, http://courtneydefeo.com/courage-for-teens.
7. Kay Wyma, *Cleaning House* (Colorado Springs: WaterBrook, 2012), 4.
8. Mother Teresa, *Where There Is Love, There Is God* (New York: Doubleday Religion, 2010), 290.
9. Mark Merrill, "10 Ways to Teach Your Children Humility," *All Pro Dad,* www.allprodad.com/top10/parenting/10-ways-to-teach-your-children-humility.
10. Ann Voskamp, "15 Happy Ways to Teach Kids to Be Grateful," *A Holy Experience,* www.aholyexperience.com/2012/03/how-to-help-raise-grateful-kids.
11. Jeannie Cunnion, *Parenting the Wholehearted Child* (Grand Rapids: Zondervan, 2014), 26.

ABC
scripture cards

ABC Scripture Cards are comprised of 26 tastefully designed 5x7 cards. Each card features easy-to-remember Bible verses from the NIV translation. Each set comes with a storage box that includes a 5" easel to display all 26 cards or a magnet to display the card on a refrigerator. The size of the card also makes for easy framing if a more permanent display solution is desired. ABC Scripture Cards are designed for the mom's style and the child's heart. Keeping them visible and merging them into your daily routine is the key!

INCLUDES 26 (5X7) CARDS
1 WOODEN EASEL • 1 MAGNET

To order your ABC Scripture Cards, contact Magnolia Lane at 205.251.5007 or visit www.MagnoliaLaneCollection.com